WHAT'S
YOUR
BOOK?

WHAT'S YOUR BOOK?

A STEP-BY-STEP GUIDE
TO GET YOU
FROM INSPIRATION TO
PUBLISHED
AUTHOR

BROOKE WARNER

SHE WRITES PRESS

Published 2012
Printed in the United States of America
ISBN: 978-1-938314-00-1
Library of Congress Control Number: 2012948055

For information, address:
She Writes Press
1563 Solano Ave #546
Berkeley, CA 94707

To Krista, and our shared love of the written word.

Thinking Like a Butterfly

by Mark Nepo

Monday I was told I was good.
I felt relieved.
Tuesday I was ignored.
I felt invisible.
Wednesday I was snapped at.
I began to doubt myself.
On Thursday I was rejected.
Now I was afraid.
On Saturday I was thanked
for being me. My soul relaxed.
On Sunday I was left alone
till the part of me that can't
be influenced grew tired of
submitting and resisting.
Monday I was told I was good.
By Tuesday I got off the wheel.

Contents

Introduction. Why Do You Want to Write a Book? 1

Chapter 1. The Art of Becoming an Author: 11
Getting Intimate with Your Category,
Competition, and Audience

Chapter 2. Anyone Can Do It: 51
Getting Over the Six Most Common Hurdles
to Becoming a Published Author

Chapter 3. Challenging Your Mindset: 89
How Challenging What You Believe Will
Help You Accomplish Your Goals

Chapter 4. The Almighty Author Platform: 127
Understanding How and Why to Build
Your Platform So You Can Prevent Rejections
and Sell More Books

Chapter 5. Your Publishing Plan: 177
A Strategic Road Map to Becoming
a Published Author

Resources 225

About the Author 231

Introduction.
Why Do You Want to Write a Book?

Allow yourself to imagine that you're sitting there with your published book in your hands. How does it feel? You are a published author. What does that title give you? What does it mean to you to have completed and published a book?

If you can allow yourself to really be in this vision of you as a published author, it probably feels pretty damn good. Many people share the goal of writing a book. Most writers are aspiring authors, hoping to one day write something that helps or impacts people; that provides a little extra income; that gives bragging rights; that allows for more books to be written and published down the road; that builds connections, community, and visibility.

Whatever your reasons for wanting to write a book, connect with them right here, right now. Knowing why you want to write a book is as important as doing it. When I start working with a new writing client, the first question I ask is: Why do you want to write this book? Sometimes people break down and cry, telling me that writing a book is something they've wanted to do for as long as they can remember. Others come with the very straightforward goal of wanting to make money. For most memoirists, the motivation stems from needing to give voice to a personal story. The business owners I work with understand that a book will bring them new clients, legitimacy in their field, and speaking gigs.

There is no wrong answer to this question. If you want to write a book to be famous, good for you. If you want to write a book to leave a legacy for your children, that's as good a reason. If you want to write a book because you have an idea that won't leave you alone, you're in good company, too. Many writers just like you aspire to write a book to fulfill a calling: to write the book they feel they're meant to write. One of my very first clients came to me with an idea for a novel she'd been toiling with for ten years. She had the first chapter mapped out perfectly in her mind. She knew the protagonist well—her likes, her motivations, her reactions. But she was stuck when it came to the details of the protagonist's love interest. She couldn't get into his mind. It was difficult for her to give him the attention he needed in order to become a full character in her mind. And so she got stuck in Chapter 2—for a whole decade.

After we had worked together for nearly two years, she completed her manuscript and sold it to an agent within two weeks. That agent has since sold the book to two overseas publishers. For the author, finishing this novel was the culmination of a dream, and she's now working on her second novel. Before we started working together, she was a woman with an idea, and today she calls herself a published author.

PUBLISHING IN THE NEW MILLENNIUM

I started working in publishing in early 2000, and since that time I've witnessed more changes in the industry than probably took place over the course of the entire century leading up to the new millennium. Anyone who follows what's happening in book publishing knows about some of these changes: the redefinition of books in the digital age; the advent of e-books, followed by their skyrocketing sales as a result of e-readers, like the Kindle, the Nook, and the iPad. This massive redefinition and overhaul came with growing pains for the industry. Like lots of industries with deep roots and particular value systems, publishing was slow to react. People who got into the industry for the love of books had a hard time wrapping their minds around how a book could be a book if it wasn't printed. Many people believed that print books were going to meet their demise as a result of e-publishing. In the early 2000s, the majority of the people I worked with felt like the apocalypse was right around the corner.

But guess what? The digital age has not destroyed publishing. It's just reinvented it. Now anyone can become a published author by self-publishing. This has its pros and cons, of course. There will always be writers who churn out crap, who write and publish books without hiring an editor or who never bother to consult with designers to ensure that the final product has the elements a book should have—things like a copyright page, a table of contents, and running heads. Professional designers will ensure that the book looks aesthetically pleasing too! It is, after all, a work of art. But for those students of what makes a good book, who want to learn and are willing to spend a little money to have a professional-grade product, publishing a great book is now possible without having to deal with gatekeepers, rejection, and unbearably long production schedules.

Of course, the gatekeepers still hold valuable roles. I was one of those gatekeepers for thirteen years, and I took my job very seriously. As an acquiring editor for two different houses (first North Atlantic Books and then Seal Press, both in Berkeley, California), I knew good writing when I saw it. I had high standards and understood what an author and a book needed to have in order to compete in the marketplace. These are the kinds of assessments editors make, even though they're admittedly subjective. Unless we're talking about an established author like Stephen King or Alice Walker, or a famous personality like Kobe Bryant or Nicole Richie, no one knows what's going to sell. Predicting how well a book is going to do is based solely on how well other books like it have done in the market and what an author is bringing to the table with their own marketing and publicity—their platform. One of the bestselling projects I bought during my time at Seal Press was a book called *The Nonrunner's Marathon Guide for Women*. A mouthful, right? None of our sales reps thought the book would amount to much when we first presented our list of titles that season. More than a few of them insisted we change the title. But the book went on to become a consistent top-of-the-list seller for over five years, which goes to show that even book industry professionals don't always know what's going to work.

Chapter 5 goes into a lot more detail about publishing—your options, what you need to do to prepare to get published while you're still writing, and insider tips. I'm one of those optimistic people who believe that anyone who tries hard enough and has enough tenacity can get published by a traditional publisher. Most people simply don't have the tolerance for the amount of rejection that can be involved in getting there. Some of you, undoubtedly, will get an agent or a publisher right out of the gate. For others, especially those with more niche projects, finding the right publisher is like panning for gold. If you stick with it long enough, it may happen, but you're going to be tempted to give up more than a few times.

I chose to self-publish this book for a lot of reasons. I'm using this book specifically as a platform-builder for my business and as a tool for my clients. I wanted and needed to get this book out by a certain date, and I wasn't interested in waiting around for a publisher's timeline. I also wanted complete creative control—something you have to give up when you publish on a traditional press.

In Chapter 1, we'll be looking at figuring out what kind of author you are—and why it matters. I'm an entrepreneur, so for someone like me, self-publishing makes a lot of sense. Once a manuscript is complete, it can be published and printed by a self-publisher in a matter of weeks. If I were pursuing a traditional publishing route, I would finish my manuscript and then write a book proposal. After that, I'd start shopping the book around to an agent.

After weeks of trying to secure someone (and after inevitable rejections), I'd land with an agent who would want to suggest changes to my manuscript. Once we were both on the same page and the proposal and manuscript were ready to shop, the agent would begin shopping my book to a publisher. Even under the best possible circumstances, if an editor picked up my book in the first round of shopping, it would be at least six months, but probably a year, before my book would be slated for publication. So rather than reading this book right now, you would be reading it approximately a year from now.

But publishing and publishing goals are unique to the individual author, and as a veteran of the publishing industry, I'm all for publishing on traditional presses. It's exciting. It's a big deal. And you can make serious money. Sometimes. So have fun with Chapter 1 and figuring out what kind of writer you are and what you want.

And then you can follow my road map to getting published in Chapter 5. No matter what, you come out a published author!

FROM INSPIRATION TO PUBLISHED AUTHOR

Chances are, you're stuck somewhere. It might have to do with time pressures and familial commitments. You've probably heard the voice of one or two of your personal saboteurs telling you all the reasons why writing your book isn't a good idea. *No one is going to read it! It's too much work! You're not a "real" writer. You suck!* If you're familiar with any of these messages, then you know these saboteurs can be real bastards. What's holding you back might be something you don't even understand. Like why you simply can't bring yourself to write that damn book, or why every time you sit down at your computer you're overwhelmed by fatigue. But don't worry—you don't have to go to therapy to figure it out. You are not alone!

Although it can be hard to confront the reasons you get stuck, I tend to like to shine a spotlight on those very things. I challenge the writers I work with from time to time to get them to see things a little differently— occasionally to think how a publisher thinks, occasionally to broaden their perspective of what they think is possible, and occasionally to call them out or call them forth for the purpose of pointing out the roadblocks that are standing in the way of their getting done what they say they want to get done. I'm making a point of saying this here in the introduction just in case there comes a prickly point where you see your procrastination, your excuses, your mindset laid bare. There will come a point when you think, *Oh my god, she's talking about me.* But this only points to just how universal some of these struggles are. Writing is both a luxury and a calling for people, which means it gets wrapped up with all kinds of personal baggage—it's the thing we don't prioritize, that can feel indulgent, that we don't own, *and* it's the thing we can't not do, that nags at us when we ignore it, that fulfills us more than most other pursuits. So, yes, it's understandable that our writing gets saddled with a lot of conflicting emotions.

In Chapter 2, we're going to examine the five most common hurdles writers face while writing their books—or thinking about writing their books. I bet one or two will resonate with you. Plus, we're going to take a look at some strategies to get you moving through those stuck places and on your way to a complete book.

Another issue we're going to tackle, in Chapter 3, is your mindset. This is both similar to and different from the hurdles you might be facing. Yes, your mindset can be a hurdle, but your mindset is actually bigger than a hurdle. It's your entire orientation to your work, and some of you are going to need to press the reset button. We're going to get you in the writer mindset so you can accomplish what you say you want to accomplish. We're going to talk about priorities and owning your writing and talking about yourself as a writer and your writing as your work. It's going to change the way you think about yourself, and it will change the way you write as a result.

The goal of this book is to help you help yourself. It's to help you get from idea—or wherever you are in the writing process—to published author. It's also to load you up with information I've learned from my career in book publishing and working with authors. If you've ever wanted to write a book and second-guessed yourself, keep reading. If you're writing a book and have a partial manuscript, keep reading. If you have a finished manuscript that you've shopped and given up on, keep reading. If you're a seasoned author with another book idea or book in progress, keep reading. No matter where you are in the process, this book will point you in interesting directions and help you figure out a few things you don't know—whether that's what your book is going to be, why you're not writing, what publishing option is right for you, or how to fully own your identity as an author. I'm looking forward to working with you. Now let's get a move on.

Chapter 1.
The Art of Becoming an Author:
Getting Intimate with Your Category, Competition, and Audience

My career in book publishing has given me the distinct privilege of having spent my adult life surrounded by authors and aspiring authors. But it's not only at work that I encounter writers. When I'm out at social events, or even when I meet another mom at the park, the conversation often goes something like this:

New person: *What do you do?*

Me: *I'm in book publishing.*

New person: *Really, wow. How cool. I'm writing a book.*

There have been times when it's seemed that everyone I meet is writing a book. And sometimes I wonder, *Is everyone writing a book?* Maybe you've wondered this, too, and allowed the little worm of discouragement to wiggle its way through your brain at the thought of so many books. So much competition! But rather than letting discouragement or intimidation get the best of you, let's take a look at where you are on the book-writing spectrum. Imagine a straight line. On one far end are those people who have an idea for a book, who have thought of writing a book or want to write a book but haven't yet started. On the other far end are prolifically published authors. They're an elite bunch, true, but they're still on the spectrum. Everyone in between either has started to write, has a few chapters completed, has a finished manuscript, has a book in production, or has one book published and aspires to write more. Where are you?

If you've even thought about writing a book, you're on the spectrum. You're just squished way over to one side, and the value you're placing on your writing is a little sliver compared with everything else you have going on in your life. Even my mom is on the spectrum. She occasionally talks about books she wants to write. She's brilliant and has enough ideas and content for four or five books, but she's way down on the idea side of the spectrum because there are a lot of things standing in the way of bringing those ideas from inspiration to publication: time, follow-through, other priorities.

There are a few invisible dividers on this spectrum, too. Past the idea people are those who have actually made writing a practice. These are people who take their writing seriously, who have found ways to incorporate it into their lives. Yet another divider is the one that separates aspiring authors from published authors. And there are a lot of published authors, which is why that elite, prolific group who've published more than a few books or who write for a living have something akin to a private reserved area on the spectrum, kind of like a members-only club.

But even publishing one book propels you past the divide and into a special area on the spectrum—and a special area in our culture. Books are culturally and socially valuable for what they say about you, for the legitimacy they lend. Being in print is prestigious, and today almost everyone in a position of power has a book—presidents (current and former), professional athletes, actors, business leaders, academics.

Some people find writing a book to be easy. They decide they're going to do it, and that's what they do. Others jump from one side of the spectrum to the other with support. They hire ghostwriters and have the resources to put together a team to shepherd their book into print. And these authors aren't any less respectable for having approached their goal to get published in this way. Others are going to struggle. It's what they do, and it's part of the creative process. For these aspiring authors, the journey is as valuable as the reward, but sometimes they can end up getting stuck in that midrange of the spectrum for longer than they might have imagined when they first set out to write a book.

So now that you've identified where you are on the spectrum, where do you want to be? Assuming that everyone who's reading this book wants to be hanging out with the published authors, good news: This chapter is all about the prep work and understanding you need to get there. You are going to find out how to get what you want by knowing what you want. Once you're clear that you have the right tools to get published, I'm going to equip you with the information you need to position yourself for success.

Getting the writing done is obviously the first and most

important piece of becoming an author, but it's far from the only thing you need to be thinking about if you want to be a published author. And I'm not talking about building your author platform. Remember, that gets its own chapter—Chapter 4. In this case, I'm talking about knowing who's come before you—your competition, your colleagues, your co-experts—and having a strong understanding of whom you're writing for. Without a firm grasp on your category, your competition, and your audience, you're cutting your book off at the knees before you even try to give it legs. If you want to publish on a traditional press, this knowledge is considered industry savvy, and it will help ensure that you get the deal you're going after. If you are self-publishing, it's equally important because readers are as valuable (more so, actually) as industry gatekeepers. Not only do you have to cater to your readers, you have to get them, speak to them, and deliver to them. And that's an impossible thing to do if you're not keeping them in mind from the very beginning.

Being equipped with this kind of knowledge is the equivalent of powering up in a video game. You're on a journey that requires some support along the way. For most of you, it's not always going to be smooth sailing. It's a process that's rewarding because of the challenge. It requires stamina, and knowing that you have these few extra boosters in your back pocket will give you strength and conviction when you feel tired or need to be reminded what you're doing this for.

WHAT DO YOU WANT?

What do you want? This is a simple question. We're asked what we want dozens of times a day. What do you want to eat? What do you want to do? What do you want to say? But when it comes to really important things in our lives, sometimes the answers can be a little elusive. Or sometimes we're embarrassed by the answers. Many women I know are embarrassed to want too much or to want too big. Lots of people think that dreaming too big is egotistical, so they censor their desires and keep themselves small.

I have long loved the quote by David Whyte that says, "Anyone or anything that does not bring you alive is too small for you." Dreaming big and holding yourself big are very distinct from having a big ego, or needing to make others less than or worse so that you can succeed. People who hold themselves big get what they want because they enter into their pursuits knowing they have something to offer. I'm a fan of *Top Chef,* and I most admire the contestants who approach every challenge with a can-do attitude and a desire to do their best, even when they have immunity. Those who rise to the top never win at someone else's expense. And it's the same in the publishing world. Anyone else's successes can be treated as evidence that books are selling and that there's a readership for your book. Others' failures can point to ways in which you can improve by not repeating the same mistakes. Holding yourself big is not about holding yourself better. It's knowing that you're putting forward your best effort and your best product, and that all that matters is giving your readers the absolute best experience you can possibly offer through your words, your teachings, your story, your message.

Does this resonate with you? Do you come to your writing as your best self? When you sit down to write, are you tapped into why you want to write the book you're writing? It's important to connect with your big self because this is the part of you that needs to show up when you sit down to write. This is the part of you that soars and has something to offer. In the introduction, I asked you to connect to the reasons you want to write, and I shared some of the things I've heard repeated over and over by authors over the years: to fulfill a calling, to make money, to build a platform, to become famous, to heal, to help, to give voice, to pay witness, to leave a legacy, to document, to get speaking gigs, to become an expert. Now tune into your big self and consider or reconsider your top five reasons for wanting to write your book. It's okay if making money and selling books are still at the top of your list! This is not about denying your ego. It's about understanding your motivations so you can make them work for you, rather than against you. List your top five reasons here:

_____

_____

_____

_____

_____

_____

_____

_____

_____

_____

Now take a look at your list. It says something about your motivations, values, and ambitions. It will also likely highlight for you which publishing option is a good fit for you. We'll revisit the connection between your values and ambitions and your publishing path in Chapter 5. For now, the value of this list is that it connects you to what you want, and knowing what you want from this process is key to committing to your writing and finishing your book.

I encourage you to post your list close to your writing space to remind you why you're writing and why you want to be published. Having a tangible reminder that's right there when you go to write can be a huge support, especially on days when you're feeling less motivated. Another reason to be able to name what you want from this process is to connect you to being a writer, which is the point of this chapter. To be a writer you must be writing, and some would say ultimately publishing. But first you must define yourself as an author. With your list to remind you why you're doing what you're doing, the next piece of work is to say you're a writer every day—to yourself, to your family, to your friends, and colleagues. There's nothing as motivating as telling people you're a writer and that you're writing a book.

When I decided I was going to write this book, I announced my intention to do so on my blog, on Facebook, and on Twitter. When the first month went by and I'd completed less than what I'd hoped to accomplish, I had to fess up. And what happened? The next month was much more successful, and I was able to accomplish that month's goal, plus make up for where I'd slacked during the first month. Before I wrote a book, I considered myself a writer, but taking on a book project was a whole new enterprise. It's challenging to write a book, and it can sometimes be equally challenging to tell people you're a writer and that you're writing a book.

So test it out, and establish a realistic goal for yourself around your writing. For those just starting out, I recommend three days a week for two or three hours a day. I personally wrote this book while raising a toddler, so my schedule was five days a week for an hour or two in the early mornings (with lots of coffee!) before he woke up. You have to do what works for you, but there's nothing like a growing word count to give you the encouragement that you're on your way. And there's nothing like giving voice to what you're doing to give you confidence and motivation to keep going.

WHERE DOES YOUR BOOK BELONG?

I once co-led a writing workshop with a marketing expert who opened with an interactive exercise that involved getting the writers in the room to figure out their category and stand with their fellow genre-mates. This started out fairly easy for most. The novelists were pleased to be partnered with the other novelists in the group. The nonfiction people found each other and even started to pair off by like category—the how-to people were in a small circle and the memoirists in another. Once everyone was standing in their circle, however, the work of truly identifying category began. Within the fiction group there were writers of young-adult fiction, commercial fiction, literary fiction, and genre fiction. The memoirists were also writing quite different books. A handful were writing misery memoir, and one was turning her blog into a book. Among the prescriptive how-to authors were so many variations that it took a while to identify where everyone was supposed to be. At the end of the day, most of the writers were surprised to find out how specific their category really was when they looked around the room at the majority of their fellow writers standing alone by category: spirituality, lifestyle, business, health, travel, fantasy, women's commercial fiction, etc.

You might be wondering: Why does this matter? Why do you need to drill down past your umbrella category to be *this* specific? It matters because it means something to the publishing industry in a very overt way, and to readers more subtly. When you go to a bookstore you know, of course, that books are organized by shelf into "shelving categories." Some readers like to browse in certain areas or know what they've come in looking for—a book on running a business, a memoir, or a diet book. Other readers are going onto Amazon and searching for a topic. They might type into the Amazon search field something like "lose weight fast," or "spiritual awakening," or "emotional abuse."

How your potential and future readers search for things should impact how you think about your book. Your shelving category points to how to title and subtitle your book, too. For literary memoirists and novelists, trends show that whimsical or illustrative titles work just fine. But for prescriptive writers, a straightforward title that helps readers find your work can directly influence sales. When considering my own title, for instance, I wanted something encouraging. *What's Your Book?* implies that every potential reader has a book in them, which is part of my message. In the subtitle, *A Step-by-Step Guide to Get You from Inspiration to Published Author,* I have key words that readers might search or be drawn to. The phrase "published author" is something that Amazon browsers wanting to publish may very well search.

You can drill down even further with this exercise by using Google's Keywords Tool at adwords.google.com/select/KeywordToolExternal (or just by Googling "keyword tool"). A search of the phrase "published author" shows 110,000 global monthly searches. The competition is "low," which is a good thing because it means the Internet isn't too flooded with people writing about topics that match this exact phrase, so I have a fighting chance of being seen or turning up in a search. Alternately, the phrase "write a book" had over two million global monthly searches, and the competition is high. This doesn't mean I should change my title or subtitle to include the phrase "write a book." In fact, it shows the opposite. There are too many searches of that phrase. You're better off in the sweet spot: fifty thousand to one hundred thousand hits.

Shelving category points as much to how you're seen as it does to who your readership is—and again, this is why it matters so much to publishers. Publishers are very concerned with "positioning," which simply means taking into consideration where your book belongs in the marketplace and how it will be perceived by your customers, fans, and buyers. If you're self-publishing, you are the publisher, so understanding how publishers think about categories is part of your learning curve. Defining what you're writing in this very specific way is in fact a function of marketing and is not editorial at all. Authors who get very tied to their title and don't think about the bigger picture do themselves a huge disservice. At Seal Press, a longtime and favorite author of mine was putting together a groundbreaking work of senior erotica. Initially, we were focused on finding a title that would showcase the fact that the book was for seniors, and we entertained titles like *Slow Sizzle* or *Aroused at Our Age*. But these didn't settle well with our sales team, and we decided we needed to look at the wide genre of well-selling books out on the market and how they're titled. We ended up with the title *Ageless Erotica,* and in doing so I believe we did a service to the book, and to readers as well.

Now, let's return to that shelving category exercise we opened with. We're going to take a deeper look at the umbrella categories that exist so that you can place your-self among your competition and better understand your audience, your competition, and ultimately your market-ing strategy. You might bridge two of the categories listed below, and that's allowed! Maybe you're a novelist with a couple nonfiction ideas, or a self-help author who'd like to write a novel one day. There's nothing inherently prob-lematic about wanting to write across categories, although it does merit a conversation (see Chapter 4) about how to manage your platform so that you're sending a consistent message out into the world about who you are. But for now, focus on the one book at hand, the one you most want to write or most need to finish—and then you can use this exercise again down the road for any future books.

Fiction

Novels are the oldest and most established book format around. If you're an aspiring novelist, you have an active imagination and a calling to write about something you know, but you don't want to be held to the facts. Within fiction, your work might be literary or commercial. Subgenres of fiction include young adult, fiction, fantasy, mystery (including cozies), thriller, and science fiction. Other forms of fiction are short stories, novellas, and erotica.

What's the difference between literary and commercial writing? On his blog, *The Writing Place,* literary agent Nathan Bransford posts, "In commercial fiction the plot tends to happen above the surface and in literary fiction the plot tends to happen beneath the surface." I like this explanation for its simplicity. I'd also add that it has to do with prose and the kind of writing readers want to read. Literary work is often more dense. It can sometimes be more flowery, ornate, or complex. Consider the meaning of the word *literary* according to *Merriam-Webster:*

> **1. a :** of, relating to, or having the characteristics of humane learning or literature; **b :** bookish; **c :** of or relating to books. **2. a :** well-read **b :** of or relating to authors or scholars or to their professions.

Now, by contrast, let's look at the definition of *commercial:*

> **1. a (1) :** occupied with or engaged in commerce or work intended for commerce; **(2) :** producing artistic work of low standards for quick market success; **2 a :** viewed with regard to profit; **b :** designed for a large market; **3 :** emphasizing skills and subjects useful in business; **4 :** supported by advertisers.

This pretty much sums up the difference. Literary work is bookish. The novel *A Single Man* (made into a movie by Tom Ford), by Christopher Isherwood, comes to mind. Anything by Toni Morrison. She's a great example of a literary author with commercial success. Popular commercial fiction, by contrast, doesn't feel bookish. These are what people are talking about when they're looking for "summer reading." They feel more like watching a movie. They're fast-paced and plot-driven. Consider a work like *The Devil Wears Prada* (also made into a popular movie, starring Meryl Streep), by Lauren Weisberger, or anything by Danielle Steel, Jodi Picoult, and other masters of commercial fiction.

When agents say they're looking for commercial fiction, they really mean they're looking for fiction that sells. Why literary fiction is difficult to sell has everything to do with readers. Readers want fun, light, dramatic reads. The general tolerance for character-driven, beautifully written, but perhaps difficult-to-get-into books is not particularly high. Of course, you have the occasional breakout, and you never know which books are going to transcend. But as a rule of thumb, literary fiction is hard to sell, and many agents and publishing houses do reject books for the sole reason that the work is "too literary."

Memoir

Memoir has been a fast-growing publishing category for years, and a controversial one, too. Memoirs are supposed to be true, and yet it's understood that memoirists take creative license. Not only are composite characters expected in memoir, they're often recommended in order to avoid lawsuits.

Memoirs are commercial or literary, too. There's an argument to be made that good memoir has plot, just like fiction, but the difference between literary and commercial memoir lies mostly in relatability. Literary memoir is still about the writing, but even more about the prose, and generally feels more "bookish." Famous literary memoirs are Frank McCourt's *Angela's Ashes* and Mary Karr's *The Liars' Club*. These are books that are as much about the writing as they are about the story. Commercial memoir, on the other hand, is more about the story and is sometimes salable because of its shock value, which explains the wide-spread popularity of misery memoir. Misery memoir is any kind of memoir that is about having suffered a hard life—and living to tell about it, or having survived it. It includes abuse, addiction, dysfunctional family, and disease memoirs. Its popularity can be attributed either to people's wanting to read reflections of people who have suffered and overcome, or to the growing trend of our voyeuristic culture and the desire to have a window into a life defined by hardship. Books on addiction and eating disorders and growing up in dysfunctional homes consistently round out the list of misery memoir top sellers (see sidebar).

However, given my experience over years of reading misery memoir pitches and proposals, I must insert a word of warning here about the genre. A lot of people are driven to write memoir because they've overcome something horrible—a family situation, early abuse, a serious addiction, a crazy mother. As an acquiring editor at Seal Press, I saw multiple misery memoir proposals a week. My word of warning is not to go overboard. Books that try to showcase too much misery can slide down the slippery slope into being undesirable. And it's a fine line. Misery sells, but despondency does not.

I saw many proposals by authors who led with lines like "This is *The Glass Castle, Lit,* and *The Kiss* all rolled into one." The proposal would then go on to detail a crazy upbringing, incest, alcoholism, and the inevitable being turned out onto the streets and/or period of promiscuity that followed. I want to be clear here that I'm not discounting how tragic these stories are, or the authors' need to get

Bestselling Misery Memoirs

The Tender Bar: A Memoir, by J. R. Moehringer (Hyperion, 2006)

Beautiful Boy: A Father's Journey Through His Son's Addiction, by David Sheff (Houghton Mifflin, 2009)

Scar Tissue, by Anthony Kiedis (Hyperion, 2005)

Lit: A Memoir, by Mary Karr (HarperCollins, 2010)

The Glass Castle, by Jeannette Walls (Simon & Schuster, 2006)

Running with Scissors, by Augusten Burroughs (Macmillan, 2003)

Dry: A Memoir, by Augusten Burroughs (Macmillan, 2004)

Tweak: Growing up on Methamphetamines, by Nic Sheff (Simon & Schuster, 2009)

This Boy's Life: A Memoir, by Tobias Wolff (Grove Press, 2000)

Look Me in the Eye: My Life with Asperger's, by John Elder Robison (Random House, 2008)

Jesus Land: A Memoir, by Julia Scheeres (Counterpoint, 2006)

Drinking: A Love Story, by Caroline Knapp (Random House, 1997)

A Stolen Life: A Memoir, by Jaycee Dugard (Simon & Schuster, 2011)

A Paper Life, by Tatum O'Neal (HarperCollins, 2004)

Wishful Drinking, by Carrie Fisher (Simon & Schuster, 2010)

Unbearable Lightness: A Story of Loss and Gain, by Portia de Rossi (Simon & Schuster, 2010) their stories out, but the impact they have on a reader is that they feel exploitative. So it's important to remember that the reason misery memoir does well is that it taps into human experience. Readers, even voyeuristic ones, are also compassionate. They want to be touched. They want to feel. These memoirs veer off-course when the author tries to showcase how horrible it all was, rather than tapping into the deeper, more universal truths and lessons that might be offered up as a result of having experienced or lived through something so tragic. Every time I rejected a book with too much going on, I wished I could tell the author that they had enough of a story without needing to pitch it like a made-for-TV drama. These are the kinds of rejections that agents and editors seldom give you, though. So consider the advice across the board: It's always about the truth of the story and your ability to touch your readers through what you've experienced and what you know as a result.

Other kinds of memoirs exist beyond misery, of course. Popular examples include food, travel, dating, yearlong experiments, and political memoir. Books like these sometimes get double categorized by a publisher, so you might see a category listing on the back of a book that reads "Food/Memoir" or "Memoir/Travel." Some publishers don't put their categories on the back of the book, but you can always find them on the copyright page with the CIP (Cataloging in Publication) data, which is category and content information provided to publishers by the Library of Congress. This data can and should inform your own understanding of your category. Having a theme-driven memoir is generally considered a plus in the publishing industry because it helps publishers position (which, to repeat, has to do with the process of understanding, in advance, how they are going to go about marketing, publicizing, and selling) your work.

Creative Nonfiction

Creative nonfiction writers include those of you writing something that's between fiction and nonfiction. Perhaps it's historical fiction, where you're writing your book through the point of view of a dead family member. Perhaps you're writing true crime, made famous and legitimate by Truman Capote when he established the genre with *In Cold Blood*. Creative nonfiction writers use elements of fiction and nonfiction in their stories, and pull equally from real life as they do from their imagination.

When trying to determine your shelving category here, you will be thinking about your competition and where they're shelved. Some of this work will be shelved in fiction, although it may have true elements. Other books might be shelved in memoir. It's largely dependent on how you choose to position the work. Yes, this word again! Publishing is obsessed with it, so it's good to wrap your mind around what it means now. In this case, it means considering the lens through which you want readers to see. If you want readers to know your book is mostly fiction, you'll express that through your subtitle, back-cover content, or category; if it's nonfiction, you'll do the same.

An interesting example of a creative nonfiction book

whose author decided to intentionally genre-bend is *Half Broke Horses: A True-Life Novel,* by *Glass Castle* author Jeannette Walls. In this case, you can see that the author and the publisher decided to showcase how the book has elements of both fiction and nonfiction, and the impact is immediate. The category is obvious, although it spans two genres and two shelves.

Increasingly, creative nonfiction is becoming a catchall for memoirists who want to bend the truth and novelists who feel that their work is too true to be characterized as fiction. For a long time, the publishing industry has held a fast and steady line about truth in memoir. Truth in fiction, meanwhile, has been treated like a secret that people can't wait to let out of the bag. Did you *hear* that John Irving's novel *Last Night in Twisted River* was based on his own life story? Of course, most memoir is based on personal experience, and people's desire to break rules and write the story they're wanting to tell without restrictions has meant that creative nonfiction has gained growing allegiance from both writers and readers.

In the aftermath of the James Frey scandal, in which Oprah Winfrey publicly chastised Frey in 2006 for having lied about how true his memoir, *A Million Little Pieces,* actually was, the book publishing world and everyone who published memoir seemed to implode. At the time I remember thinking, *Yeah, but that was a really good book.* And it is. It's a well-written story. Fast-paced. A good read. We now know that Frey's publisher pressured him to turn his novel into a memoir. You can put yourself in his position, I'm sure. A publisher says, "We love your book, but we can't publish it as fiction. How much of it is true?" Add on to this conversation whatever amount of money was being offered for an advance, and you can probably see yourself in Frey's shoes.

This many years later, the publishing industry is perhaps a little more careful, but also, I think, more open to publishing genre-bending work and to finding ways around the problem of fiction-memoir blends by doing things like subtitling a work *A True-Life Novel*.

Prescriptive

If you're writing a how-to book, you're writing a prescriptive book. For prescriptive writers, structure is king—and often points to inspiration for your subtitle. For instance, you might decide to structure your book around a formula: *7 Steps to Clearing Your Clutter for Good; 30 Days to the Best Health of Your Life; 100 Tips for Saving Money in the New Economy;* or, in this book's case, you're reading *A Step-by-Step Guide*.

Writing a prescriptive book requires you to show up for your reader in a way that's very different from what's expected of novelists, memoirists, and creative nonfiction writers. You are expected to deliver advice and content that shows readers how to do something. You need to be a trusted guide, teacher, or expert. Books in this genre are really about how to do anything—quilt, start an online business, fix your car, tile your bathroom, build a birdhouse, declutter your life, write a book!

Titling and subtitling in this genre is a very

straightforward exercise. As we discussed above, use key-words and don't try to be too clever. Let your subtitle do the heavy lifting of showcasing what your book delivers. Your category is always going to be prescriptive in these cases, but you want to make sure to look at your toughest competition and figure out where they're shelved first. For instance, if you're writing a book on how to run a business, your category is business, not how-to. Similarly, if you're doing a book on how to make jewelry from home, your category is going to be craft.

If you're not sure what your category is, turning to your competition is the easiest way to figure it out. If their categories are not listed on the back covers, remember to check the copyright page. If you don't find anything helpful there, another good way to figure out your category is to search around on Amazon and look at the books under the heading "Customers Who Bought This Item Also Bought." This sometimes points you to the author's previous works, or books that aren't particularly relevant, but it more often directs you to work that's in a similar vein, and it can be very helpful when assessing this question of where your book belongs.

For those of you who are self-publishing for the purpose of gaining more exposure or to sell your book to your existing or future clients, shelving category is still something that's worth being aware of. Knowing that I have a prescriptive book about writing and publishing will help me when I'm ready to pitch my book to reviewers, and when I'm ready to spend promotional dollars. Your shelving category gives you key words if you ever choose to make use of pay-per-click advertising online. If you end up shopping your book to a publisher, positioning yourself in the correct category is key.

All of this work goes toward being in the know. It's good to speak the industry language when you approach your future agent, publisher, or reviewers, and to know what you want when considering advertising opportunities. If I were pitching my own book, for instance, I would tell a reviewer that I have a prescriptive book for aspiring authors that covers everything they need to know to get published. Knowing your category and your positioning helps you make a clean and clear pitch. Coupled with understanding comparative titles, which we're covering in the next section, you'll be using industry-speak and get better results across the board.

GET COMPETITIVE AND COMPARATIVE

For aspiring authors, getting comfortable with their competition is a critical order of business. Doing competitive title research on your book is in fact an important first step in the writing process itself. More important than that, however, is understanding what competitive and comparative mean in the context of book publishing.

Many people have a negative association with competition. It's intimidating. It sends a shot of anxiety straight to their core. Comparing yourself to another person might not feel good either. It's reminiscent of middle school—he has nicer arms than you do; she has better hair. If these are the kinds of images and memories that come up for you

The Pitch

In book publishing, you pitch your work to an agent; you pitch your work to editors; and you pitch your work to reviewers, sellers, buyers, and anyone else who will listen. Lots of writers' conferences these days hold what are called Pitch Fests, for the purpose of perfecting the pitch. And while it's true that the pitch is important, if you don't have the content or the chops to deliver on the promise of a great pitch, you still won't get the deal.

So, what do you need to know in order to pitch? In addition to giving a paragraph description of your work and saying a little bit about yourself as an author and why you're the best person to write this book (or to have written it), you can also using shelving category to your advantage. Consider the following examples:

- There are countless books on the market about how to run a small business, but none of them shows you, step by step, how to go from being an online retailer to starting a brick-and-mortar shop. This book is a combination of *The Online Business Survival Guide* and *Start Your Own Business*, two strong sellers that speak to my same target audience.

- This book spans two bestselling categories: food and running. Readers have been flocking to food memoir and running books for years, and in this book, the author tackles eating, cooking, and all things food from the perspective of a hardcore athlete who needs and loves to eat.

- In the vein of the popular novel *Girl, Interrupted* comes a memoir by Jane Doe that showcases what rehab looks like today. The success of James Frey's *A Million Little Pieces* demonstrates that there's an appetite for books that showcase a behind-the-scenes look at this world. Nicole Johns's *Purge* investigated rehab from the point of view of a woman with an eating disorder, but Doe's book is about hardcore treatment, sparing no one and taking a decidedly dispassionate point of view on a subject that will engage readers.

These kinds of openings are what are called "hooks." They capture the attention of the person on the other side (agent, editor, reviewer) because they point to shelving category and competition—two of the key concepts you need to understand in order to appropriately position your book.

when you think of competition and comparing, it's time to reframe. Please join me for a little competitive and comparative title boot camp.

Considering your competition is a must. You cannot shop your book without having done competitive title research. ("Shopping your book" is how you'll refer to sending your book out to agents or editors—essentially meaning that you are looking for representation.)

The following are common things authors do that you should never do, followed by some best practices to reframe how you think about competition:

1. Don't ever say there is nothing like your book on the market.

Reframe: Competition shows publishers that there's a readership for your book. I believe that writers feel compelled to say that there's no competition because they feel worried that existing books on the same subject will make their book seem less desirable. But in fact, the opposite is the case. Book publishers use competitive titles to justify buying a book for their list. They are looking at topics that sell well and deciding to move forward based on sales of previously published, similar, or like-minded books.

If you have a book that crosses two genres, like the food-and-running book mentioned above in the Pitch sidebar, you can break your competitive title list into two categories. It's okay to say that there's not another book that approaches the subject of running from the vantage point of food and cooking, and then to showcase the most popular food memoirs and most popular running books. This is a double whammy, since it will effectively prove to the publisher that both categories are good sellers and your book appeals to both markets.

2. Don't ever compare yourself or your book to the current number 1 bestseller or the ultra-famous.

In the mid-2000s, every other funny proposal I got was from an author claiming to be the next David Sedaris, and boy, did that get old fast. In the late '00s and into the 2010s, every single travel book, adventure book, or woman-going-anything-alone book was the next *Eat, Pray, Love*. Agents and editors are looking at book proposals every single day, so doing your comp title research and choosing books that are truly on par with what you have to offer goes a long way. You can even reach for a person you aspire to be like. For instance, if you're a travel writer, maybe you choose a couple of Bill Bryson books. Or if you do spirituality, maybe you want to compare yourself to Wayne Dyer. To me these are authors who are successful, but not so successful that it's inconceivable that another human could reach their level of success. Alternately, comparing yourself to Oprah or President Obama or Paris Hilton (all published authors) doesn't serve you. You want to be impressive, but also grounded.

3. Don't ever go into deep detail about how bad one of your competitive titles is.

If you create a nonfiction book proposal, you're charged with the task of listing your competitive titles and creating a summary statement about how your book is different. Some authors take this opportunity to slam the competition and show only how their book is better. This is not the point of this exercise. Going off on a very well-selling book is not something that editors particularly love to see. This is not a review. It's an opportunity to explain how your book is similar to and different from its competition. The ways in which it's similar may point to reasons why another book like the one you're writing is needed. How it's different will hopefully make a case for a publisher to take on your book, because some aspect of what you're doing is unique. By following the standard protocol of a proposal and giving an analysis of the competition, you are helping the publisher say yes to your book. Competitive title analysis is a very straightforward exercise. Remember that publishers use it as a tool, and your job is to make their job easy.

Okay, boot camp is over. But I do feel passionately about the value of the reframing—obviously. I've just seen too many aspiring authors make the mistakes I've listed above. And the impact is that they look like they don't know what they're doing. The way to succeed in publishing is to scoop up all the insider knowledge you can get and approach the whole prospect of becoming an author like you would go about applying for a job you really want. You do research on the company. You come with a portfolio. You come appropriately dressed. You speak the language.

All of this works to your advantage because book publishing, no matter whom you're working with, is about long-lasting relationships. The people you're collaborating with have to work with you for years to come, and you in turn have to work with them. People want to like each other, right? People on the book publishing side like to work with veterans because they've been through the process, so they know what they're doing and they're easier to work with. This is not to say that you can't raise your hand for help, or that you're not going to need a little hand-holding, but comporting yourself in an organized and savvy way will make agents and editors want to work with you. And that, my friends, is the key to getting your foot in the door.

And for you self-published authors who don't give a lick about agents or editors, again, understanding the competition matters. You can ask your competitors to endorse or review your book. Perhaps this won't work if someone is a direct competitor and endorsing one another will send a mixed message, but in the case of memoir and novels, this is never the case. Readers have a huge appetite for good stories, so if someone who's written in your same genre will endorse you, then their readers will hopefully find your book. When I was working on a book for Seal Press called *Bento Box in the Heartland,* a memoir by a Japanese-American woman who grew up in the Midwest, we searched high and wide for other Asian Americans who had written coming-of-age memoirs. These writers endorsed my author, and she in turn endorsed them. The idea here is that an Asian American readership may well like to read more than one experience about what it's like to grow up between two cultures.

This is yet another reframe because it's taking the idea that your competition is your enemy and turning that around to instead think about ways in which your competition can help you, and you can help your competition. A few authors I've considered to be my competition for this book are Jeff VanderMeer, author of a book I absolutely adore called *Booklife: Strategies and Survival Tips for the 21st-Century Author,* and Ariel Gore, a former Seal author and author of the book *How to Become a Famous Author Before You're Dead.* If either of these authors approached me to endorse their book, I would jump at the opportunity, of course. And even though they're my "competition," I do believe that someone who read *Booklife* would benefit from my book, and I won't stop referring my clients to either of these books just because I'm hoping to hoard all those sales for myself.

I'm of the belief that the more expansive and inviting you can be, the more opportunities you will have— for endorsements, for reviews, for getting published, for sales. Approaching your competition from a place of abundance over scarcity will help you in the long run because we cannot control the fact that more books than ever are getting published. According to Wikipedia, 288,355 new titles and editions were published in the United States in 2009 alone. Other online search results show the number of new titles per year to be hovering in the one hundred thousand range. So, wow! No matter what, that's a lot of books. Your only job when putting a new book on the market is to engage your readers and draw upon your networks. And giving your competitors a few high fives along the way not only makes you feel good about yourself but can help you in ways you might not even be able to conceive of just yet!

Before we close out Comparative Titles 101, I want to give a few genre-specific tips on how to think about your competition and how to make it work for you in your query letter (to agents or editors), your pitch (to reviewers and media), your proposal (for nonfiction writers only), or your solicitations (for endorsements and mutual backscratching).

Fiction

As mentioned above, decide whose work your writing most resembles. If you have a hard time discerning this for yourself, ask your friends to read your work and tell you if your writing reminds them of anyone. Or hire a well-read editor to give you an assessment of your writing style. Ask them whether your writing reminds them of a published author or authors they might know. If you are in a writing group, ask your fellow members for their feelings or opinions to this effect.

If you intend to shop your novel to an agent or publishing house, you will use this information in your query letter. If your work truly resembles that of a well-published author, try to get an endorsement from someone who's willing to say so. Consider including a blurb in your query letter, though it should be from someone sort of well known, even if it's just someone who's been published before. A blurb is an endorsement, and it could read something like this: "This story is more jaw-dropping than *Running with Scissors*. I couldn't put the book down! It's the kind of story that stays with you long after you're done." Eye-catching, right? Agents and editors will think so, too.

Memoir

A comprehensive list of competitive titles and title analysis is required for memoir. Where relevant, break your competition into categories. You might do this if you have an issue-based or topic-driven memoir, or if your memoir spans two categories.

Just like with fiction, use competitive titles and authors in your query letter and pitches. You might say that your writing style is similar to Caroline Knapp's, or that your memoir is similar to Alice Sebold's *Lucky*. It's okay to use known memoirs, but you wouldn't want to compare your memoir to Nelson Mandela's. Giving specific names and memoir titles helps agents and editors get into a certain frame of mind for reading your work—but of course, you do need to deliver. So, again, if you can't assess your own writing in this way, find someone who can.

Creative Nonfiction

Like memoir, this is a well-established category, and finding suitable competitive titles should not be too difficult an exercise. When thinking about the authors who hang out in this pool, however, think about your contemporaries. *In Cold Blood,* though the most famous example of true crime, is not a good competitive title because it's too old and too much of a classic.

For those of you writing in this genre, feel free to step outside of creative nonfiction and use fiction and memoir titles as comparative titles. It's going to be difficult and limiting if you feel you must stay within the confines of other creative nonfiction, and this is already a rather amorphous and constantly changing category.

Prescriptive

The prescriptive writers are likely to be the ones who feel that their competition is more direct and can therefore be more on guard around this whole reframing thing. And that's fine. I get it. For instance, if you're the best-known Fabergé egg designer in the country and you've written a book on the topic, you might bristle when the next up-and-coming designer comes along with a book of their own. You might decide that endorsing them is a conflict of interest or a bad business decision. I am not claiming to be an expert on super-niche businesses, so you'll have to make this decision for yourself.

However, if you're in a broader category, like finance or small business or publishing, chances are that your competitors' books are not going to preclude sales of your books. Chances are that you can cross-promote each other's books and enter into a mutually beneficial relationship. It's possible, for instance, that I will contact Jeff VanderMeer and ask him to endorse my book. In exchange, I will post a link to his book on the resource page of my website and continue to talk up his book to my clients—and my feeling is this will not have an adverse impact on my book. It's good karma, and if Jeff likes my book, maybe he'll recommend it to his readers, too.

Like I've said previously in this chapter, look for your competition among those authors who are at the level you aspire to be at. This is driving home the point I've been making that it's better to compare yourself to someone whose success you can actually hope to achieve, be on par with, or perhaps even surpass, but not someone who's a household name.

WITHOUT READERS, YOU'VE GOT NOTHING

I cannot overstate the value of narrowing down your readership so that you can wrap your mind around whom you are writing to and for. You are not writing for everyone! A common publishing industry refrain is, "Do not try to be all things to all people." The more you can narrow down and position your work as appropriate to a specific subset of readers, the more likely you will be to get the attention of an agent or editor.

So how do you figure out whom you're writing for if you don't already know? Think about who would benefit from your book. Consider who your ideal reader would be. List five people you know who you'd love to have read your book once it's finished. They can be a specific person, a type of customer, or just your ideal reader. A couple of examples I came up with for myself include:

- First-time authors who specifically come to their projects from a place of inspiration, passion, drive, and even longing.

- Any writer who's been sitting with an idea for a book for a year or more.

- Writers interested in the difference between traditional publishing and self-publishing.

I'm sure I could come up with a handful of other examples, but let's focus on whom I'm not trying to cater to:

- Already published authors. (Yes, if they find my book and want to learn what they don't know, perhaps, they're welcome! But they're not my target audience.)

- People who don't want to write a book. (This one may seem obvious, but if you decide that "all women" or "all men" or "everyone" is your target readership, you are, in effect, making a similar kind of mistake: specifically including in your readership people who wouldn't be interested in your book.)

Your turn:

For those of you writing memoir, your target audience might feel a little elusive at first. Most writers of prescriptive books know exactly whom they're appealing to: their customers—people who want to learn how to do what they're offering to teach or show or exemplify in their book. For memoirists, it might be worthwhile to think about the kind of person who would not read your book. For instance, if you were writing a memoir that talked about an abortion you had in college, followed by your feminist awakening, you can probably determine that right-wing Republicans are not your target readership. If you are a male author writing a spiritual memoir about how overcoming your fears and angers allowed you to better connect with women, you shouldn't try to have women be your target readership. You want to be thinking about those guys you're writing for in this case, envisioning them as your support system while you write. Your invisible target readership can act like your cheering section while you're writing, and they can help you write a better book.

Look to the sidebar for a few other target audience samples. Ultimately, if you shop your book to a traditional publisher, you will need to include a target audience section in your book proposal. If you do this exercise early, before you start writing, you will have this list at your disposal, saving yourself the effort later. I recommend bullet points because they're fast and easy. You can visualize a particular subset and let them work for you—both now while you're writing and later once you're shopping, or once your book is out.

The other reason to know your target readership is for post-publication reasons. Yes, they're your cheering section while you're writing (or they can be if you let them be), but they're also the invisible masses who want your book. If you can pinpoint them now, once it comes time to develop a marketing strategy, you'll know how to reach them. If your target readership is everyone, where do you start? If your target readership is cupcake lovers, you know you can start with cupcake bloggers and owners of cupcake shops. You will seek out cupcake contests, conventions, and other aficionados. You will not be inadvertently trying to reach women who are dieting.

Target Audience Samples

Target audience for a book about addiction
   -Parents dealing with teen drug addiction
   -Parents dealing with teen alcoholism
   -Parents of teenagers and young adults
   -Parents of young adults with addiction issues
   -Concerned family members and friends of families
    struggling with addiction
   -Individuals in twelve-step or other recovery programs
   -Addiction counselors
   -Psychologists
   -Hospitals and treatment centers
   -At-risk teenagers or young adults
   -Teachers and other school officials
   -Anyone who has been affected by addiction

Target audience for a book about choosing not to have children
   -Those aged twenty-five to sixty years who are childless and are uncertain whether or not to have children, or have already made the choice to be child-free.
   -The millions of voluntarily childless in North America.

Target audience for a book about boomers taking on exciting challenges
   -The potential audience for this book is the thirty-nine million baby boomer women in the United

States between the ages of forty-five and sixty-five. Their generation has an estimated spending power of $1 trillion, according to a report by MetLife.

Target audience for a book about divorce and sex

- Divorced and separated women and mothers of all ages, but particularly those over thirty.
- Women who enjoy reading about sex or hidden desires, or women who watch shows like *Cougar Town*, *Sex and the City*, *Desperate Housewives*, *Hung*, and *The Real Housewives of Orange County*.

If your target readership is people who have overcome a difficult set of circumstances (which is a typical subset of people certain memoirs try to reach), this exercise of figuring out your target readership can get a little more nuanced. How old are you, and what demographic do you hope to reach? What kinds of experiences are you bringing to the table, and who would benefit most from what you are sharing? Do you have a desire to help others through your book? Who are those people you'd like to help? Once you've figured this out (ideally before you start writing or while you're writing), then allow these parameters to continue to inform how you reach people. Look to organizations that help the same kinds of people you want to help.

If you're writing about spiritual awakening, look to spiritual centers and magazines and blogs that cover those topics. If you're writing about having been abused in some capacity as a child or young adult, look to shelters, to resources for survivors, to other authors who have published into this category. Don't forget, as I mentioned above, that your competing titles can be your best allies. If you've had an experience similar to something another author has written about, reach out and see if there might be an opportunity for cross-promotion. The worst thing that can happen is that the author will say no, but at least you've made them aware of your book.

Straight to the Presses

If you've been doing the exercises I've been prompting you to do in this chapter, I have good news for you: Much of your query letter and your eventual nonfiction book proposal will be developed from the concepts this chapter covers. This chapter has been about prep work, much of it groundwork that can help you visualize your final product and what you want to be thinking about once the book is out.

I have a dear friend, a coaching colleague and author, Sara Connell, who does an exercise called Future Pull with her clients. In it she encourages her clients to visualize their success beyond their wildest dreams. Where publishing is concerned, aspiring authors would lean into the future and experience their book being published and available for readers. They would speak as if these things have already happened, and feel the power of their success and accomplishment.

This entire chapter is in some ways a Future Pull exercise, in that it's an invitation to think now about what you want your book to be. You will benefit tremendously from understanding and knowing what you want, where your book belongs on the shelf, and who your competition and readership are. All of this gets you thinking like an experienced author, or thinking like a publisher. If you want to get published, your book has to be more than just "good enough." If it's your first book, it sets the tone for all subsequent books you will ever write. If it's your legacy book and the only book you'll ever publish, it needs to be something you'll feel proud of. Whether you end up publishing on a traditional press or self-publishing, your standards for what you hope to achieve should be the same. And all of this prep work lends itself to your creating the absolute best book you're capable of.

For those of you who've longed to write a book for years, all of the prep work can serve as structures to actually get the work done. When I sat down and created my book files for this book (you can watch a webinar tutorial on this at youtube.com/warnercoaching), it made my book real. Even though there was no content in my documents, the fact that they were labeled "Chapter1.doc," "Chapter2. doc," etc., served as a reminder that these chapters were sitting there, ready to be written—and no one but me could make that happen.

For those of you who are just starting to think about writing a book, educating yourself on the process and figuring out the right approach is going to be your first consideration. We are going to cover the various possibilities and paths to publishing in Chapter 4, but I can't stress enough how much you'll be aided in the process if you nail down the concepts covered in this chapter—your shelving category, competition, and audience—before you go any further. If you haven't completed the exercises, go back and do them, even if it's fast and in pencil so you can change your answers later.

With this work set in place, take a second to visualize your book. If you're artistic, you can even create a mock-up of your book cover and keep it in your writing space for inspiration. If you have a title or working title, say it out loud. Imagine now walking into the bookstore. Walk to the shelf where you know your book will be sitting, face out, of course. Or maybe it's on the front table when you walk in, or on an aisle endcap. Take a note of the books surrounding it—the friendly competition. Now look around at the other people standing in the aisle. These are your readers, your target audience. Take it all in. This is your future.

Chapter 2.
Anyone Can Do It:
Getting Over the Six Most Common
Hurdles to Becoming a Published Author

There are several classes of writers: those thinking about writing a book they haven't started, those thinking about revisiting a book they've stopped writing, and those writing a book. Depending on where you are in your process, your hurdles are going to look a lot different—of course. For those in the inspiration or idea phase, there's the work of getting the content on the page; for those wanting and needing to revisit an already started project, there are inevitably inner-critic messages to contend with; for those in the throes of writing, there may be a question of knowing when it's done, or how to get it published once it is complete.

This chapter is about hurdles that present themselves in the writing process, but it's important that we take a second to visualize what a hurdle is. It's something to be overcome or jump over. Maybe because I ran track in high school, this metaphor has always been particularly vivid. Unlike a professional hurdling event, in high school there are lots of kids who go out for hurdles who have to learn how to jump over them. They're barriers at first—things to overcome—but once it clicks, the runners seem to glide over the hurdles, and their approach to and getting over the hurdle are part of their natural stride.

It's the same for the hurdles that present themselves in writing. Published writers know how to glide over them. Beginner writers facing them for the first time have a learning curve to contend with. Writers stuck at any given stage of their writing are just like the hurdler who goes down at hurdle number 4 but must get back up in order to finish the race. She must get past that hurdle and keep going. It's possible she'll nick others on her way to the finish line; it's even possible that she'll fall down again. But for many hurdlers like this, fear of falling again makes them forfeit the race. When it comes to getting published, you are going to fall, and it doesn't matter whether you win; you only need to get to the finish line.

In this chapter, we will be taking a look at the hurdles on the road to getting published. You're going to glide right past some of them. They might not seem like a big deal to you or like something you'll ever have to contend with. Others may seem insurmountable, or you'll recognize them as an obstacle, something you dread having to figure out. In every case, pay attention to the strategies for getting over the hurdles. And don't just think about them. Do them.

1. SABOTEURS

Saboteur is my preferred word for the inner critic, and *saboteurs*, plural, show up for us when we write in a number of ways. Any judgment, fear, resentment, envy, or self-doubt you have in your life outside of writing will show up for you when you start to write. All the things you try to stuff down, avoid, ignore, or be better than will niggle their way into your writing process at some point. This is because writing exposes us. Writing is an expression of who we are. Whether you are writing a novel, a memoir, or a prescriptive how-to, your words are on the page, and the ultimate goal is not just to be read, but to be understood, to be liked.

You can recognize your saboteurs by their messages:

- You don't know what you're doing.
- Who cares?
- Why are you bothering?
- We have better things to do.
- Memoirs are self-indulgent.
- This story sucks.
- No one is going to want to read this.
- This is such a competitive category. How am I ever going to get published?

Sometimes saboteurs show up without a voice and manifest themselves in your energy. It can feel like lethargy; it can take the form of pride or an "I'm better than." Consider the writer who justifies to herself that she can't write because she's being a good mother. The message is: *I prioritize my parenting, and no one can fault me for that.* But this, too, is a form of self-sabotage, because what it says is that you and your writing are not as important as everything else in your life.

I can't think of a single writer I've worked with who hasn't dealt with the saboteur on some level. For memoirists, a saboteur can express itself in what other people will think of your writing. It's the saboteur who encourages you to write under a pseudonym. Saboteurs are self-protective. And they're a part of you. So make no mistake: They want to keep you safe. But in keeping you safe, in protecting the status quo, they are also keeping you small. If you are compelled to write your truth (in any form), then the truth wants to be out. But the saboteur's message, often, is that telling the truth will hurt. It will hurt you. It will hurt others. Remember that these are messages that have been drilled into us from a very young age. Don't tell. Be polite. No one wants to hear about that.

Identifying the source of your saboteur's message is important, because often what you'll discover is messaging from your family of origin. Another word for the inner critic is *superego*. To get psychological on you for a brief moment, the superego is one-third of the theoretical construct, identified by Sigmund Freud, that also includes the ego and the id. The superego is the part of the mind that deals with criticism and morality. But the superego is also the parental part of us. It's the aspect of our minds that keeps us in check but also aims for perfection. Those of you struggling with the notion that your book or writing has to be perfect are probably contending with a pretty powerful superego.

The thing about the superego—and therefore all saboteurs (which are really just a way of breaking out the various messages of the superego)—is that everyone's experience of it varies. I remember that when I first started studying the Diamond Approach, I believed I didn't have a very strong superego. The ego resonated more strongly with me. As a kid, I didn't have authority figures who squelched me, who told me not to tell, who said or implied I wasn't good enough. So, with my strong sense of determination and self-confidence, I figured I was one of the lucky ones who'd gotten to adulthood fairly unbruised. Wrong! What I discovered is that I had found ways to placate my superego. It was getting exactly what it wanted, but subtly. My superego was busy busy busy keeping everything in check, everything on task, endeavoring every single day to maintain the environment I'd worked so hard to create.

For me, since I was working in publishing, my superego was the voice that said, *You don't have to write a book. You work with books every day.* Every once in a while someone would ask if I was a writer, and my pat response was, "No, and I don't really have the desire to write." I specifically remember telling someone that working with writers made me realize that I was better suited to be an editor. Seeing the talent that was out there, I decided that I was better off staying small, better off doing what I did in the background and supporting other people's dreams.

The process of writing this book has brought saboteurs out of the woodwork. They're the peanut gallery desperate for an audience—but we don't have to give in. What's encouraging is that the more you write, the more their voices fade into the background. Saboteurs, after all, cannot compete with being in flow. Any of you who've experienced being "in flow" know exactly what this feels like. The words come more quickly than you can type them. You know exactly what you want to say, and you're inspired. It's exciting! You feel *alive!* Saboteurs cannot even attempt to compete with these feelings, because they're the exact kind of emotions that set you free from your critics. These are the emotions of authenticity, freedom, being present, and allowing yourself to soar. Here you are unencumbered, fully engaged in creation.

There's no time or space for saboteurs here because flow is you in the current. It is speedy and edgy and dangerous and thrilling. By the time you see your saboteur, you're already a half-mile down the rapids. *So long, old friend!* If you happen to catch a note of its nasty song—*you can't do this, you're not good enough, this sucks!*—it doesn't matter, because the words are indecipherable against the rush of the wind and the expansiveness of your soul.

Strategies for Overcoming the Saboteur Hurdle

I imagine as you've read this section that the old, familiar voice of the saboteur has inserted itself once or twice, if only to say, *Uh-oh, they're about to turn a light on me.* So yes, go ahead and do this. List three things your saboteur might say or has said about your writing or your desire to write:

_____

_____

_____

_____

Now, what is there in these messages that feels like it's about trying to keep you small? Can you identify anything in what the saboteur is saying that might be about trying to protect you? Can you see how the message *your writing sucks* might in fact lead you to the conclusion "If you don't put it out there, you won't get hurt"?

Next, spend a moment identifying your saboteur. If you can easily identify more than one, great. Do this exercise for each of them.

- Is it a she, a he, or an it?
- Identify any smells, textures, colors, or associations you have with it.
- Give it a name. Rickie, Burly, Black Bear, and Goo are some names my clients have come up with for their saboteurs.

Once your saboteur is identified as a she, he, or it; once you have a sense of what it looks like; and once it has a name, spend a moment really looking at it. Ask your saboteur what it wants from you. What it needs from you. As I've said above, time and time again I've worked with clients to figure out that their saboteur almost always has one primary motive: self-protection. Self-preservation. So befriend this voice and work with it. Give it a reassuring pat on the back. No, you're not going to play it safe, and you are going to be okay. Acknowledging it and giving it some space allows you to move easily through its messages, rather than willpowering your way through by ignoring it or falling victim to what it has to say.

Exercises

Once you've identified your saboteur, here are a few fun things you can do, depending on how much power it holds over you:

Create a poster board with all its messages. Make it big and bold and put it somewhere visible. Remember, your saboteur just wants to be acknowledged, and sometimes seeing its messages in big bold letters can help you see just how ridiculous and over the top your saboteur really is.

Make it real. If your saboteur is green or red or associated with some other color, mix some Jell-O (the saboteur's color, of course) into some water and put it in a jar with a lid. Label it "saboteur" or the actual name of your saboteur. Place it in the fridge or the freezer. You can do this any time you feel like your saboteur is too much in your space. It's an effective way to capture it and remind yourself that you have control over when it shows up and what it has to say.

2. TIME BANDITS

Time bandits come in all forms. They're anything that keeps us from doing what we commit to doing where our writing is concerned. They might be social commitments. They're most certainly work commitments. They can show up as the guilt we feel for not spending time with

our family. They can also be the many other personal commitments we have: exercising, mowing the lawn, doing the
dishes. There are a few lucky individuals who have figured
out lifestyles that foster having a creative life, but most
people struggle to find the time in their schedules to write
a book.

Looking at your existing commitments as time bandits
is not meant to shame you or make you feel like you should
be giving up on something else in order to write your book.
After all, we have to pay the bills. We want and need to
spend time with our families. However, time is slippery,
and any time is not a good writing time. If time is an issue
for you, you must schedule your writing. Do not let your
writing be something you'll get to, or something that's on
your to-do list every day. The notion that every day *may
be* a writing day usually manifests as guilt for not doing
enough writing—or any writing. Weeks and months can go
by like this. I've seen it many, many times: writers who feel
guilty every day for months—even years!—for the writing
they're not doing.

Strategies for Overcoming the Time Bandit Hurdle

The number one and only strategy here is scheduling your
writing time. But along with scheduling comes honoring
your writing enough to keep your appointments. You must
block them out in your calendar as you would any other
appointment. How likely are you to miss your kid's doc-
tor's appointment that you scheduled two months ago? Or

your lunch date with an old friend from college whom you haven't seen in years? Not very likely, right? These writing appointments need to be things you won't break. And until you prioritize your writing as you would these kinds of appointments, you'll find that time bandits will be an ongoing issue in your writing life.

Getting serious about your writing means showing up and doing it consistently. For those of you without a regular writing practice, I recommend what I call the "3 x 3 writing schedule." This is three hours a day, three times a week. It doesn't matter when you schedule this time. When I was writing this book I was doing it from 4:30 a.m. to 7:30 a.m., before my son woke up! For others it might need to be after the kids go to bed, or on Sundays, or during the lunch hour. If you can't work in 3 x 3, do what you can. Maybe it's 1 x 5, but whatever it is, make it consistent and put it in your calendar.

Another important way to overcome this particular hurdle is to enroll your family and friends. Tell everyone in your life that you are writing a book, and let them know how important it is to you. I have worked with many authors who didn't get serious about their deadlines until after they had a book deal. Very few of you have that luxury, however. Most of you are going to be working to finish your book before you secure a publishing contract, or if you're working to finish a book that you're self-publishing, then it's all on you. Don't get sucked into needing outside validation as a motivator. Become your own taskmaster, and get support from your family and friends. You can even use them as accountability partners who help remind you when you are not keeping appointments with yourself or when you're inadvertently or self-indulgently allowing your time bandits to keep you from writing.

Exercises

Get a writing gym partner. Find someone who's going to care whether or not you show up to write. On She Writes.com, you can find someone in a heartbeat. Here's what you set up with your partner:

- Permission to send them emails when you start writing and when you sign off.
- Permission not to respond to every email, or you probably won't have a partner for too long.

The point is not that they respond and cheerlead you. The point is to be accountable to someone other than yourself. There is power in those emails. Try it and see.

Write down all your excuses for not writing. For not writing as much as you want to. Seriously, write them down. For instance: I have too much to do; I have to pick up and drop off three kids at three different schools; I'm tired of my book project right now; I had to go grocery shopping; the toilet was grossing me out all week. When you see what you write, you will see your priorities staring you in the face. Some things should take priority over your writing, and other things shouldn't. Consider what you're taking on that you don't have to take on, and try to move one thing off your list. And it's good if you write something down that's a full-blown excuse—something that you feel a little embarrassed about. The point of this exercise is to take ownership of why you don't write, or don't write as much as you want to. The more truthful you are, the more eye-opening it is.

Pay yourself for showing up to your writing sessions. I'm dead serious. We all know the power of money. It doesn't work to charge yourself for missing a writing session, because then you're collecting on yourself, but it **does** work to figure out a payment system for doing your writing. These can be small amounts that lead up to being able to treat yourself to dinner once a month, or if you have a business associated with your writing (which you should!), then you, author, can pay your writing business, and then write off payments to yourself as legitimate business expenses. Talk about lining yourself up with steady work!

Start a "treadmill journal." I stole this one from Gregory Martin (www.unm.edu/~gmartin), and I suggest it to my clients all the time. You just keep a little journal by your writing space, or on your phone, even, and enter the following five things:

1. Date and time
2. How long you will work
3. What you plan to work on
4. How it went (and I would add how many words you wrote)
5. What you plan to work on tomorrow

Sample entry:
1. November 15, 2011, 11 a.m.
2. Write until 1 p.m.
3. Working on love scene between Phoebe and Serg—Chapter 3, Scene 4.
4. It was hard. I suck at writing love scenes. But I still wrote 1,500 words in two hours.
5. Tomorrow, 8–10 a.m. Will start Chapter 4. Yay.

Tip: Keep it this simple or you won't keep doing it. And use it to keep track of your time and hold yourself accountable.

Turn off your Internet, email, and phone. All systems down. There is nothing more distracting than feeling the compulsion to check email or check for a text. If you're worried about an emergency, tell your kid's school or partner to call your landline. If you don't have a landline, get one. It's worth the $10 per month to keep you on task. This one may seem obvious, but I know how hard it is. And turning everything off has to become something you do for yourself that's similar to freezing a credit card you need to stop using. Sometimes we have to be our own drill sergeants. And the payoff is worth it.

3. YOU DON'T KNOW WHAT YOU DON'T KNOW

When it comes to writing and publishing a book, there are a lot of big questions and concerns writers face. Is my content well organized? Will it resonate with my audience? Do I have a point-of-view problem? Are my characters consistent? Are my anecdotes helpful? Do I have too many anecdotes? Does my structure make sense? We've all read lots and lots of books, but when we sit down to write our own, it's not as if we're able to translate the experience of reading a book into executing our own book. Sometimes writers don't confront these questions as they write. They're so content with their process and self-confident in their writing that it's only once they start getting rejections and questioning why this is happening that they start to get concerned about whether there might be something they're not seeing. What is it that they don't know?

I like to coach writers from the point of idea or inspiration, rather than once a manuscript is complete, because there are so many opportunities in this kind of collaborative relationship to ask questions and develop something truly masterful as the writing unfolds. It's not to say that mastery doesn't happen without someone else's eyes on your work, but for a lot of writers, this collaborative process of working with an editor or a coach is key to being able to see what they don't know. You want to find someone who can work alongside you and bring onto the page what you think you're bringing onto the page. The likelihood you're not seeing what's missing is fairly high—particularly if you're writing a memoir or a novel that you're very close to.

Many writers get stuck right in the middle of their manuscript. This is what my colleague Linda Joy Myers, president of the National Association of Memoir Writers, calls the "murky middle"—that place smack-dab in the middle of your work where things start to get muddled and difficult. Writers are notorious for not being able to see the forest through the trees, and this most often happens because they're not working from an outline, or because they don't have a particularly disciplined writing practice and they're writing their book over a long period of time. Imagine what it would feel like to watch a movie over a two-year period. Do you think you might need to go back and rewind the video a few times to refresh your memory about what happened? The same is true with your own writing, of course. It's difficult to just dip right in and pick up where you left off—even if it's only been two or three weeks since your last writing session.

When you're deep in the writing, it's often the most

rewarding place you can be, and also the most difficult place to maintain perspective. This lack of perspective I see in writers is why I'm so insistent about outlines. Outlines help you see the view from ten thousand miles above. It can feel daunting to outline an unwritten book, and time and time again I see creative writers insist that outlining impedes their creative process somehow because they don't know what's going to happen yet. My response to this is to give permission for your outline to be a working, living, breathing document. It gets to change and morph as you write your story, but you have to know where it's going. So often I'll be sucked into a particular TV series—usually a drama—and it's so good for a few seasons. Then all of a sudden it's clear that the writers have lost their way. It's equivalent to being in the murky middle. The show will start to get unrealistic, the characters inconsistent, and eventually the show will get canceled, or I'll stop watching it before that. This is what happens when you don't map out your book: You get to the middle and you start looking for solutions, rather than having thought this out in advance. Don't trick yourself into believing that it's better not to know, and to let the characters or the plot speak to you as you write. This may have worked for a novelist or memoirist you admire, but it's not something to emulate.

Down the road, whether you're just starting out or almost finished with your manuscript, you will share your work with friends or professionals. You will likely shop your work to agents or editors, unless you intend to self-publish. When this happens and you put your work into a public space, you will start to get conflicting feedback. This can be difficult for writers because questions invariably arise around what to do with that feedback. This is where I will caution you. Listen to your instincts. Make sure the feedback resonates with you. Find a coach or an editor who gets you. This is key! If an agent or in-house editor gives you feedback, don't rush to fix your book according to their opinions. I can recall at least three occasions during my time at Seal when I was interested in a book project but something was off. When I approached these authors with my editorial vision for their book, it turned out that what I was suggesting had been their plan all along, but they'd been advised somewhere along the way—by a well-meaning friend, a writing partner, their agent—to change the book.

This is not an admonition to be rigid. I'm actually a huge advocate of flexibility and collaboration, but you must learn to trust your inner knowing. If you're urged to change something to make it more commercial or more salable, make sure that you're going to be happy taking your book in that direction. I firmly believe that every book knows what it wants to be. Sometimes authors try to squeeze their book into a different mold to satisfy someone else or to sell their book. There are countless examples of this happening, and sometimes the results are positive. Maybe a book becomes a bestseller and the author never regrets it. But more often it's the case that the author knows they tried to make the book something it wasn't supposed to be. The most infamous example of this is James Frey, who knew he had a novel but agreed, on the advice of others, to sell *A Million Little Pieces* as a memoir. I've worked with a number of authors over the years who felt pressured into writing a book they didn't want to write. This happens for any number of reasons—but most often because an agent or an editor has a vision for the book they want an author to write and then the author feels obligated to write that book, or like they *should* write that book because someone is offering them money to do so. It's very difficult in the moment to be objective if and when these offers come your way, but if you have reservations, make sure you at least explore them and talk through your options with someone you trust.

Remember that writing is subjective, even if you're writing a prescriptive book. Not everyone is going to love it. Not everyone is going to get it. Writing a book requires you to develop tough skin, especially if you expect to get reviewed. No matter what, you will receive some negative reviews. So, at the point when you finish your book, after the editing and after the proofreading, what's important is that you feel good about it. That you've had people you trust, and hopefully a few professionals, get you to the place where you know what you've done is the best you can do. Call it good and move forward. Resist the temptation to rework and rework once you've gotten to this place. It's important to know your own boundaries and to take outside feedback when it makes sense to you and not take it when it doesn't.

Strategies for Overcoming What You Don't Know

The number one solution to overcoming not knowing what you don't know is information gathering. You can start with books like this and move on to websites. There are amazing authors, coaches, and industry professionals in this space (and in every space!) who are doing great blog posts and offering up tons of information. An easy way to find them is by following someone you know of on Twitter and then seeing who follows them, or who they follow. You can quickly follow a trail of experts on any given topic.

Working with professionals, like I said, is invaluable. Find an editor you trust, or get a writing coach to bounce your ideas off of. One of the biggest differences between a coach and an editor is that a coach will explore your process with you while an editor generally tries to improve your writing and help you better articulate what you want to say. If you really want to learn how to become a better writer, a coach can help you do that. Always key is trusting your own intuition. You will know when something doesn't feel right—when an editor's feedback feels off, when a comment doesn't resonate with you, when you're feeling pressured to take your book in a direction that doesn't feel true or authentic. Yes, hindsight is twenty-twenty, so you won't always know what's happening when it's happening, but try to have the wherewithal to check in with yourself and especially to consult with your trusted team—whether these are friends or professionals.

A final solution to this problem is to join a writing group or a community of authors—in person or online. This offers an opportunity both to educate yourself and to get support. Finding out how other authors managed to finish their books and get published is inspiring and motivating. They're not so dissimilar from pregnancy stories, or war stories. Once you've been there, you have a story you want to share. It's to process what you've been through, but also to offer advice. So if you're a first-time author, listen and pay attention to all the different ways authors get published. And if you find yourself facing something you don't understand, reach out and ask!

Exercises

Outline your book! I talk about outlining ad nauseam because it's so damn important. And I'm a stickler for it. But I also love it. As a former acquiring editor who made a lot of decisions about whether to buy a book based on an outline, I speak from personal experience about its value. So yes, it's helpful to you for understanding where you've been and where you're going—giving you a snapshot of your chapters so you don't have to constantly reread where you've been or wonder where in the hell you're going next—but it's also an invaluable piece of your nonfiction book proposal. The outline sells your book because most agents and editors will not read a whole book through before taking it on. They read sample chapters to get a sense of your writing, and then rely on the outline for the arc of the entire narrative.

For you fiction writers who think you're off the hook because you don't have to provide agents and editors with a nonfiction book proposal, I have news for you: You really should! A chapter-by-chapter synopsis along with your first fifty pages can really go a long way. I equate this practice with bringing a portfolio to an interview. You don't have to, but it's impressive, and it can't hurt!

Join online communities. If you're a woman writer, join She Writes (SheWrites.com) to connect with other women writers. If you're writing a memoir, join the National Association of Memoir Writers (namw.org). Another great resource for groups is LinkedIn. Any affiliated groups of people you can possibly imagine are connecting on LinkedIn, but if you can't find something you're interested in, start your own group. You can do this on Meetup.com as well.

Sign up for newsletters. Good industry newsletters include Publishers Lunch, Shelf Awareness, and Publishers Weekly. Signing up to stay in the loop on publishing news will help you remain connected to the ongoing conversation in ways that will help you once you're ready to start exploring your publishing options. You can also sign up for newsletters from authors you admire. Another good way to find great newsletters is to go to Twitter and look to see who people are following. Generally, people with a lot of Twitter followers have those followers because they're putting out good content. I encourage you to sign up for my newsletter on my website: WarnerCoaching.com.

4. RENEGADING IT

Writers go renegade in all sorts of ways and for all sorts of reasons. I've had clients tell me they didn't think their book needed to be copyedited or proofread, only for me to go in and find pretty glaring errors. I've done strategy sessions with writers who would clearly benefit from support —coaching, a writing group, an accountability partner— but they don't gather a team. Blame it on personality, on resistance, on justifications for why it's better to write in

isolation or to try to reinvent the wheel. You're reinvent-
ing the wheel whenever you spend time and energy trying
to figure out things that other people already know a lot
about. It's similar to not knowing what you don't know,
except that it's the hurdle of stubbornness, not wanting to
spend money, or thinking that you can (or should) figure
it out.

As I've been working to grow my own business, the best
advice I've received has been around hiring other people
to do the work they're good at and to focus my own attention on what I'm good at. Unless you have tons of time
on your hands and you really like getting your hands dirty
and figuring things out, it makes sense to hire people to
help you. It makes sense to hire a team. If you could be
making, say, $30 or $40 or $70 an hour doing the work
that you do, consider what happens when you start tinker-
ing with things that you could pay someone else similar
rates to accomplish. Consider this example. You make $40
an hour doing whatever you do. Would it be valuable to
you to pay someone else $20 or $30 an hour to execute
something they have expertise in, rather than trying to
do it yourself? Think about it: You pay out $20 or $30 an
hour for the work, yes, but in that time you would be earning $40. So you might argue that you don't want to pay
someone that kind of money to do work for you, but you
could be earning $20 or $10 an hour in these scenarios
and *still* getting an hour's worth of work.

This point was finally driven home for me when I
attended a Cash Machine Workshop put on by Loral
Langemeier. She talks about outsourcing everything, but

especially housekeeping. It's been a sticking point for me for a while. My justifications for not having a housekeeper have been (a) I don't want to spend the money on something I can do for myself, and (b) I like cleaning. But in the fall of 2011, I took the plunge and hired someone. They come every two weeks, and guess what? I no longer spend all day Saturday cleaning house. I spend some of the time I would be cleaning working on my writing, or on my business. Do you think I "earn" the cost of the housekeeper? You bet I do. It costs me $100 for a team to clean my entire house in one hour, something that would take my partner and me together at least two hours. If I can put a value on my own hour of about $50–60 (and it's probably worth more than this, honestly), that's $100–120 earned, plus the two hours I didn't spend housekeeping, which would be the equivalent of $100–120 lost. And another revelation I had once the housekeepers started coming: I don't like cleaning as much as I thought I did.

Let's take another example of hiring someone else to convert your book files to epub files. At some point, if you choose to publish an ebook or self-publish, you will need to convert your Word document into epub files so that they can be read by Kindle, Nook, iPad, etc. I had this conversation with my brother when he was about to publish a Kindle-edition ebook. Rather than hire someone to do the conversion for him, he decided he wanted to figure it out himself. Now, my brother knows a lot about computers, and I'm sure it didn't take him that long to figure it out, and a case could be made that he also wanted the knowledge.

But a guy I know quoted $50 for the conversion. And so we can go back to my brother's wanting to do it himself for the challenge, and that's great, but there's no way this project took him fewer than four to five hours to figure out. So was it worth it for him to pay someone else $50 for four to five hours of his time? That very much depends on what his time is worth to him, right? And this is the very question you want to ask yourself.

I've also seen authors go renegade because of personality issues. This can get a little more complex, and it can be difficult to recognize in yourself. If you're someone who tends to rush through things and not be particularly thorough, you might fall victim to overlooking things or not caring about things that are actually important. This is a personality issue because it has to do with how you tend to work. If you can acknowledge to yourself that you tend to have a million spinning plates in the air, and that you're more of a visionary and/or less detail oriented than others, you want to be careful. Seek out support. I can't tell you how many authors I know who have shoveled out tons of money, especially in the self-publishing process, because they actively chose to rush through their projects. In one case, a woman hired me to salvage her self-published project because she'd printed a book that hadn't been proofread. Once she got advance copies of the book, she shared it with her mentor, who was quite upset with all the errors she was finding. She told the author that she had to consider how reviewers would receive the errors in her book. Your book, after all, is a reflection of you. So this woman pulled the book from Amazon, hired me to proofread it, reuploaded the files, and reprinted the book. This was a very, very expensive mistake.

You might be thinking that she should have known better. She should have gotten the book proofread. But she had gotten the book copyedited, so it's possible she thought it was in better condition than it was. She thought she could skip this step—maybe because it was too expensive, maybe because she was in a hurry to have the book release in time for a certain event, or maybe just because— who knows? But when it comes to having a professional book, there are a number of steps you need to follow. Working with people who know what they're doing will help you know which steps to follow.

Time and time again I tell my self-published authors, don't hire your daughter to copyedit, or your friend who sort of does proofreading on the side as your primary editor. It's not worth it. Your reputation is on the line. Think of it as if you were hiring someone to race your prize-winning horse. You wouldn't just pay some kid who liked horses, or a girl you met at the stable who rides on the weekends. You would hire a professional, because a lot would be at stake. It's the same with the team you hire to help you get your book published.

People also tend to go renegade because of money. Yes, deciding you want to write a book can get expensive. You can hire any or all of the following: a coach, a ghost-writer, a copyeditor, a proofreader, a designer, a printer, a third-party self-publishing company, a publicist. You'll hear about plenty of people who get published without hiring any of these people, and certainly you don't *need* to hire someone. You can attend free webinars, do research online, join a writing group, or get together with a trusted friend to discuss your writing. But consider the value of professional feedback and doing it as a gift for yourself. Again, I can't overemphasize the importance of finding out what you don't know. I have assessed one too many proposals riddled with problems written by authors who are completely befuddled as to why they're receiving rejections. Find out what you're not seeing, and your chances for getting published will increase exponentially.

Strategies for Overcoming Your Impulse to Go It Alone

The best thing you can do for yourself is to find an accountability partner. Whether this is a coach or a writing pal or a friend, you need someone who supports your writing and who can give you objective feedback. This is true whether you're in the throes of your writing, shopping around for an agent, or figuring out how to get self-published. If you have a trusted person who can call you out, you are not renegade.

For those of you who know or have a suspicion that you're a personality type who doesn't like to ask for help, you most especially need to take stock of what you might do to seek out support. Most of the authors I know who fall into this category seek help only out of desperation. They have a book they've been working on for ten or fifteen years that they really want to finish and realize that they can't or won't without support. Or they have wasted money on mistakes they could have averted. Or they've gotten rejection after rejection and they're finally taking a look at their query letter or their proposal and sample writing and wondering if maybe they could or should get an outside opinion. It's just like your health: You want to be preventative rather than reactive. Don't wait for a problem to present itself and then start CPR to salvage the mess. Seek out strategies that will prevent the mess from happening in the first place!

Exercises

Take a personality test. I recommend the Myers-Briggs Type Indicator (MBTI) or the Enneagram, both of which you can Google to find their tests. The MBTI measures a person's psychological preferences, while the Enneagram measures the ways in which a person's attention is directed. Taking a personality test is not for everyone, but if you're interested in understanding yourself and whether you might gravitate toward a style that refuses or actively resists help, a personality test can be a way to discover your strengths and hold your resistances with compassion and understanding. Sometimes when we can actively see why we resist something, it can lessen our reactivity and help us reach for supports that we wouldn't have previously been open to.

Join. Yes, simply join. Join a writing group. Sign up for a webinar. Actively participate in message boards. Listen in on free calls. If you're writing in isolation, not showing anyone your work, waiting for it to be perfect before it can see the light of day and grace your future readers with its brilliance, then you are probably a renegade. I can't tell you how many authors I've worked with who don't have a website, who refuse to do social media, and who toil away on their books convinced that when they're ready—when their book is ready—it's going to be well received by publishers and readers and make them a fortune. Wrong. This is not how it happens. The way to build interest in your book is to be a joiner. You need to have networks and know people. You need to be some-one who's savvy about the publishing industry, which is fairly easy to learn about if you just go online and read other writers' blogs. Try commenting. Like certain Facebook pages that speak to publishing-related issues. Make yourself known. You want to be the popular kid. You want to know a lot of people. You don't ever have to meet them face-to-face. That's the beauty of online com-munities. But you have to emerge from your cave and get realistic about the value of online connections.

5. GETTING YOUR BOOK SOLD

This is a big one and a hard one. Lots of writers come to me after they've been unable to sell their book, either to an agent or to a publisher, or after their agent has been unable to sell their book on their behalf. This will happen to a lot of you, and it's the reality check of traditional pub-lishing. This is more than a hurdle for some writers. For some it's the end of the road for their book project, and therefore the death of their publishing dreams.

I always ask new clients what will happen if they can't sell their book. Might they pursue self-publishing? The reason I want to know this up front is that I want to know how much skin they have in the game. There are the rare few writers who are publishing a book solely to become famous. Most writers want to publish to have their words in print, to increase their business or gain legitimacy, for the purpose of being able to say they're published, or to sell a few books (hopefully many more).

So if you're still writing your book, ask yourself this question now. What happens if your book doesn't sell? And don't fool yourself that getting an agent means that your book will sell. Getting an agent is a solid first step, and something worthy of celebrating. But it is not the same as getting a book deal. Agents have a difficult time selling to editors, too, and after some months (or sometimes years) of trying to sell a project, agents have to throw in the towel, even the most dedicated among them.

I write about this hurdle not to be discouraging, but to be clear about the business of publishing. It's a tough game, and you need to know you have options. As an advocate of self-publishing (and having self-published this book because I chose to), I like to encourage authors to be open to self-publishing as part of their overall picture of publishing. I offer the following strategy to my clients: Shop for an agent; if that doesn't work, shop directly to a publisher; and if that doesn't work, self-publish. Knowing that you have options is key.

In my audio program, *The Paths to Publishing,* I talk about these three paths—getting agented and publishing on a big house; publishing on a small house (agented or not); and self-publishing—as analogous to going to an Ivy League university, a state school, or junior college. All are viable options, and some people get a better education at a junior college than their counterparts at an Ivy. In part this is because it's all about what you make of it. It's possible to get published on Random House or Penguin and see your book completely fail: bad sales, bad reviews, your publicist not returning your calls. It's also possible that your self-published book will be met with success beyond your wildest dreams. There are plenty of examples of self-published books that have skyrocketed to national and international success, or even just modest successes that have superseded the authors' expectations. So you never know. Not even the big book publishing deal guarantees a great experience.

Strategies for Overcoming Not Being Able to Sell Your Book

There are two solid strategies here: (1) seek out the support of a good editor, or (2) self-publish. Decide what you're willing to invest and how much it means to you to be published on a traditional house. I believe that with enough work and persistence, writers can get published in today's climate. But sometimes it takes digging in with your editor, tweaking your manuscript to their liking, and/or shopping to lots and lots of agents or editors. I've seen some writers dedicate years to this process, so it's important to know your tolerance for rejection and how long you're willing to wait to have your book out in the world.

Self-publishing is more straightforward. Here you essentially opt out. You don't have to deal with someone else validating your work or telling you whether it deserves to be published, and you are in control of your content and your experience. But you can't approach this lightly. Getting your book self-published is a lot of work, and you're going to want to put some time and effort into marketing it once it comes out, or you won't sell any copies. Most self-published authors at least want to break even. More likely they want to turn a profit. This cannot happen without a website and a portal to sell the book, even if that's just a link to Amazon. You must also be engaged with social media. Create a Facebook fan page for your book. Get on Twitter and share your process, ideas, and little tidbits about your book.

Making a concerted effort to figure this stuff out grows your platform! Even if you end up selling only a few hundred copies of your self-published book, you're better positioned to either (a) traditionally publish your next book or (b) rally your existing fan base for a second book. Either way, you're further along than where you started. And that's the key thing about platform. It does take time to build. It doesn't happen overnight. You have to have content that's interesting and makes people want to check back and see what you're doing. And even figuring out how to do that is a learning curve—but a fun one if you give it time and energy.

Exercises

Get a proposal or manuscript assessment. If you've received a lot of rejections, meanwhile, and think you might suffer from the above-mentioned hurdle of renegading, it's a good idea to get a proposal and/or manuscript assessment. Don't keep sending out your proposal after multiple rejections, hoping it will get better. Stop and get help. It's possible that you still won't sell your book, but at least you'll know that you're going out with your best work.

Go to a pitch fest or writers' conference. Both pitch fests and conferences give you opportunities to come face-to-face with agents and editors. Not all of them will give you honest feedback about your work, but there are many who will. Start learning about your genre and the business of publishing. You can begin to gauge whether there's a real market for your book, and some of what might need to happen to propel you to the next level. Or it might be motivation to self-publish your first book, work on your platform, and then try to get your next book published traditionally.

Dedicate time each week to building your platform. Lack of platform is probably the number one reason, after poor writing, that proposals and manuscripts get rejected. It's difficult to hear that your writing is great but your platform isn't strong enough. It can feel like a stab in the heart, actually. Here you are, getting validation for your good work, and someone is telling you that you don't have enough fans, followers, or connections, and so they won't publish your book. But this is the way it works. So rather than get discouraged, get onboard. If you're still writing, you have a leg up. Start working on your platform now! If you've been hearing from agents and editors that you need a better platform, you have some choices to make. You can outsource platform building, though it's pretty expensive to do so. Actively working your platform yourself is also hard if you don't know what you're doing. It can take three to four months—or more—to build the necessary base, and for some writers that's too long to wait. I'm always talking about self-publishing a first book as a good way to build your platform, the reason being that it allows you to test the waters. You'll learn a lot about marketing in the process, and you automatically get an "online presence" (a key component of having a platform) by actually having an ebook or a physical book out in the world. It gives you something to talk about, promote, and sell. It's much easier to build a platform around a self-published book than around no book at all.

6. TECHNOLOGY

Technology is a big issue for a lot of writers, and it can continue to be whether you publish traditionally or self-publish. Technology is involved in building a platform, and if you're self-publishing, there's a lot you're expected to know. On the most basic level, it's important to familiarize yourself with the mechanics of Microsoft Word, because this program is the industry standard, and most publishers want you to submit your work in MS Word. Showcasing your lack of technological knowledge early on in the process is something easily avoided. Even if you don't feel comfortable with technology, you don't need to tell your prospective agent or editor. Save your technology questions for your computer-savvy friend or kids.

It's more around platform where technology can begin to trip some writers up. If you don't like social media, or email, for that matter, you're going to need a perspective shift. Five years ago, it was okay not to be on Facebook and Twitter, but today it's pretty much an expectation that you be posting, at least occasionally. Similarly, having a website or a blog used to be an added bonus. Today it's an expectation as well. Start small and free if you don't have a site already. It doesn't have to be complicated, but by the time you start shopping your work, you must have an online presence of some sort, and it behooves you to move past any resistance you might have to technology. I know a lot of people who thought they didn't like social media but ended up loving it. The bigger danger, in fact, became the time involved in maintaining a platform, rather than understanding how it all works. In my opinion, this is a better problem to have. It's easier to create boundaries around your technology use than to refuse to understand how it works.

Technology is also a big hurdle for a lot of self-published authors because some of the technology is in fact quite advanced. Some platforms are easier than others. I would argue that Lightning Source (LSI), as good and popular as it is, has one of the more difficult-to-navigate platforms. You have to feel comfortable with a certain level of technology in order to work with this company. But by and large, this is true to some degree for most of the self-publishing companies you're going to work with. If you do not feel comfortable with technology, hire someone who does—whether that's a consultant or someone who can simply help you make sure that you're following protocol. On LSI's platform, for instance, there are a lot of questions about what you want your discount to be set at and whether you want your books to be returnable. You can ask questions of your representative at LSI, but they are not consultants and they are not paid to advise you. I had a client who ended up in an exchange with her representative at LSI about returns, trying to argue that it didn't make sense for her to accept returns because she's just an author of a single book, not a company. The result was that her representative at LSI suggested she consider using another company. They are a service provider, and they don't care if their client is a big company publishing one hundred books a year or an author publishing a passion project.

Strategies for Overcoming Your Disdain for or Resistance to Technology

You can either outsource it or learn it. Like I said, you might discover you love certain aspects of technology once you start messing around with it. Social media is pretty fun, and it can be exciting to begin to build a platform, watching your number of followers and fans grow by the day.

Outsourcing your platform building is a good option for those of you who are growing a business. Growing your platform is necessary not just for your book, but for your business as well. More people can find you if you have a website that works for you and if you have social media that's focused—securing your branding and driving home your messages. If you've decided you're going to self-publish but you're overwhelmed by technology, hire a third-party self-publishing company—someone like PublishNext.com, Infinity.com, TurningStonePress.com, or SheWritesPress.com. All of these companies offer hand-holding through the self-publishing process, setting up your title, offering design services, and setting up your epublication options. Other self-publishing companies that fall into this category are the Author Solutions companies (which were purchased by Penguin in July 2012 and include Xlibris, iUniverse, Balboa Press [Hay House's self-publishing arm], and Westbow Press [Thomas Nelson's self-publishing arm], among many others). Know whether you want to go big or small, whether you want a more boutique experience or a big push-'em-through kind of experience. Do your research—just as you would when trying to understand which traditional house you want to publish on. With self-publishing, this becomes even more important because there are no barriers to entry. You get to choose who you end up with, so don't just go with the first company you happen upon. Do research, compare prices, and ask questions.

Where online-platform building is concerned, the best strategy is to start small. The two most important things you need are a website and a Facebook page. You can get a free or very low-cost website through WordPress.com or Blogger.com. Set up a site and start posting once a week, or once a month. All that matters initially is that you be consistent. For Facebook, either use your personal page as a place to talk about your writing or consider setting up a fan page or a subscription page for yourself and/or your book. These are options that allow people to like you or subscribe to your feed without friending you, meaning that you don't have to field requests or deal with people you don't know wanting personal information about you. Lots of people ask me if they should set up a Facebook page for a book they're writing if the title might ultimately change. I say yes. You can change your Facebook fan page name if fewer than two hundred people like it. So follow your own progress, but it can take a while to build up to two hundred, so don't wait just because your title isn't finalized.

Exercises

Make use of Google and YouTube! You can get tons and tons of good information about any technology and/or self-publishing platform by doing a simple Google search. People offer tutorials on YouTube about everything from how to use Word to how to start a blog. There are great sites about authors' experiences with the big self-publishing platforms—LSI, CreateSpace, and Lulu. People's blogs are tremendous and free resources. It's a lot like reading the instructions before you start putting together a complicated piece of furniture—you want to do it. I work with a lot of authors who remind me of my teenage stepson, who, when he sits down to work on his homework, starts asking questions before he even really starts *thinking* about the assignment. Rather than read and do the critical thinking necessary, he wants us to answer the questions for him. If you already know you're this type of person, remember what I said about not going it alone. Hire someone to advise you! Otherwise, do your homework. Read up. Spend time online and find the countless free resources that are out there and that exist specifically to inform you.

Create a blogging schedule. Lots of writers are overwhelmed by the idea of having to blog or do social media because it detracts from their writing. And it's true—it's a time-suck. One easy way to deal with this is to sit down and map out a blog schedule—which includes microblogging (Facebook and Twitter posts). Decide at the bare minimum what your longer blog posts are going to be about in advance so that you don't feel like you have to spend hours executing a post. Map out ten to twenty Facebook posts at a time, so that they're there and ready to go. All you have to do is upload them once a day, or three times a week. The more you can get into the habit of doing this in advance (dedicating a day or two per month to this process), the less overwhelmed you'll be. Also, if you have a Facebook fan page, link it to your Twitter account so that whatever you post to Facebook automatically gets pushed out to Twitter. You can find out how to do this by Googling it, and it's an easy way to make sure you're posting on both social media platforms.

Use Hootsuite.com, Seesmic.com, or another, similar tool. Hootsuite.com and Seesmic.com are sites that offer a service that allows you to schedule your social media posts in advance. You can schedule a week or a month ahead, load up all of your posts, and determine what days they'll go out. This is sort of like outsourcing, because once this is set up you don't have to think about your social media all week, or all month. This is an invaluable tool for the pre-planners among you, and something to consider making use of even if you're not a planner, to save yourself the effort it takes to come up with new posts every day.

Chapter 3.
Challenging Your Mindset:
How Challenging What You Believe Will Help You Accomplish Your Goals

In the last chapter, we covered the six most common hurdles to getting published. And while your mindset can be a hurdle, I think of it a bit differently—mostly because your mindset is something you have to work to challenge or change, rather than overcome. Your mindset is your orientation to your work, and while some of you might have a positive attitude and high confidence all the time, most writers find they need to press the reset button every once in a while. This whole chapter is about getting you in the writer mindset so you can accomplish what you say you want to accomplish where your writing is concerned. We're going to talk about claiming your writing as valuable, owning your writing, letting go of perfection, releasing the hold external validation has on you, and living like an author in your everyday life.

MINDSET CHALLENGE: HOW DO YOU VALUE YOUR WRITING?

Writing isn't a real career. You're a writer? Okay, but what's your real job? Writing isn't going to pay the bills.

If any of these statements resonates with you, you're the victim of having had your writing dreams squished by someone, somewhere. The impact of these kinds of messages on our writing and our writing lives is profound. It can be challenging to believe that what we have to say is valuable, or that it matters to others. When we don't value our own writing, it can be tough to make it a priority, or to justify why you need or want to spend time doing it. Likely you know deep down that it matters to you, but you're stuck with these voices—your saboteurs promoting old messages—about why you shouldn't write, why your writing is a pipe dream, or why it's not as important as other things in your life.

Unfortunately, many young writers in love with the written word hear these messages from parents or from teachers who maybe think they're doing their students a favor by introducing them to how harsh being an adult really is. You can't survive on writing alone! There are those who promote these messages out of fear, and others who truly don't have kids' best interests at heart. There are plenty of dream-killers out there who crush others because of their own insecurities, narcissism, fears, and failures.

I had my own first experience with a dream-crusher in high school. He was a popular teacher in the English department, and I was taking his AP literature class. We rarely wrote personal essays, so when we had an assignment to write about something that had informed who we were, I was excited and chose something close to my heart—a two-foot bronze Quan Yin statue my great-aunt, an artist, had created. The statue had a special place in my heart for lots of reasons—there were only four ever created, and seeing it in my grandparents' home in Tacoma, Washington, was my earliest memory. I was a sixteen-year-old with confidence in my writing ability. I was proud of my essay, and I expected to receive glowing remarks, an easy A.

To my shock, and ultimately to the detriment of any aspirations I might have had around writing, my teacher gave me a D. The essay came back marked up in red, so thick I couldn't even see my original type on the page. I wish I'd saved that assignment so I could look back at it today from an adult's point of view, from an editor's point of view. Regardless, I walked away from that experience believing that the assignment said something about me. That I couldn't write. That writing wasn't my thing. That I found my way into book publishing and have had the great privilege of midwifing many books into print has perhaps been a form of healing.

Can you recall an experience similar to mine when someone told you that your writing was frivolous, that it wouldn't pay the bills, that majoring in English was a waste of time? If so, it's important to identify it, especially if it happened early in your life. These are stories we can choose to rewrite, after all. And there are different forms of writing. I still don't aspire to be a literary writer of personal essays—and I'm not sure I can blame that on my AP literature teacher. I have, however, claimed my writing voice. And I've been able to reconnect with that confident sixteen-year-old who believed she was a good writer.

Each of us comes to the table with different messages, fears, belief systems, and values around our writing.

Writing is many things to many people—a blessing, a chore, a have-to, a gift, a challenge, an uphill battle, a reflection of the soul, our truth, a need. And I'm sure you can think of many other things it means to you. Dealing with something so complex, so nuanced, means that there are no set answers about what it should be. Writing a book is not so dissimilar to parenting. There's no manual. You figure things out as you go. It's one of the best things you do, and sometimes it makes you want to scream.

Anyone reading this book must believe somewhere deep down that writing matters—that their writing matters. And yet it's not always the case that we can equate believing our writing matters with believing that what we are writing matters. It's a subtle distinction, but some of you know exactly what I mean. You can value your writing life—knowing that writing brings you alive, defines you, is an artistic outlet—and still struggle to believe that a given piece of writing (an essay, a blog post, a book) is going to find an audience, strike a chord, make a difference.

So how do you start believing? Where do you look to align these disparate experiences? How can you believe, as strongly as you do that your writing matters to you, that it will matter to someone else?

Reconnecting with How Your Writing Feeds You

A lot of authors I've worked with over the years have been workhorses, so much so that they'd lost a lot of the joy that had brought them to writing in the first place. When it comes to valuing our writing, many of us believe that the writing should serve a purpose. You should be earning money, getting published, having something to show. Writers who get into this particular value system around their writing have usually lost whatever joy brought them to their writing in the first place. Their writing becomes something they should be doing better, differently, more effectively.

I encourage my writers to own their writing as their work (which we'll talk about a little later on in this chapter), but there's more to our writing than its simply being an extension of our work. It's also who we are—and writers who have it deeply ingrained that their writing must serve a purpose are usually disconnected from the joy, passion, and fun of it. If this is you, try to remember what originally brought you to writing. Stop to visualize the first moment you realized you loved to write. You may have been quite young. I've worked with many writers who have known they wanted to write for as long as they can remember. For others, the bug didn't hit them until high school, or until they were in their twenties. It can often be sparked by a book that changed your life, or by an experience in a bookstore or a library, or with a particular author. Consider what it was and feel what it was about that experience, or that early time in your life, that moved you, that inspired you to go to the page of your journal or to the blank screen of your computer to write.

Now consider what message—whether early or late—interrupted that inspiration and turned your writing into a should, a must, a vehicle to get you from point A to point

B. Maybe you feel that your writing isn't legitimate unless it's earning money for the household. Maybe you're dealing with the fallout from a dream-crusher, like my high school English teacher, who made you believe that your writing wasn't worthwhile. Now it's time to examine whatever that energy, feeling, or thought is that's making your writing hard work, not fun, a should.

Examine these two energies together at once. Take the moving, inspiring, full-of-wonder energy in your left hand and the heavy, should, this-is-not-fun-it's-work energy in your right. Feel the difference between them. You have a choice about how you approach your writing. Even if you write for a living, you can give yourself permission to reconnect with that early passion. Sometimes we need to remind ourselves about why we love what we do. We need to remember that our writing nourishes us and treat it more like a satisfying, luxurious meal than like quick take-out. Taking a moment before you sit with your writing to honor what you love about it is a good practice, and a good way to get connected to flow. It's like diving into your writing seamlessly and without reserve, rather than inching in laboriously and with effort.

Moving Beyond Divine Inspiration

Oh, how we can get bogged down in comparisons and belief systems around our writing. So many authors over the years have asked me, "Does every writer struggle with these issues?" "Have you ever worked with another writer who has to work as hard as I do?" Questions like these stem from some misguided belief that writing is somehow easy, or that it's supposed to just come to you. I call this "divine-inspiration thinking" because many writers get caught up in a mindset that "real" writers don't have to work as hard. Or they believe that they should write only if and when they experience that wonderful sense of flow all writers know and love. But sometimes flow is a lot like chasing the dragon. It's an experience we crave, but not all writing sessions are going to be so connecting, magical, and fulfilling. Sometimes it's going to feel hard, and that's got to be okay, too.

Any of us who write—especially those of us who write full-length book projects—know that writing is a discipline. It takes discipline to carve out the time. It takes discipline to conceptualize an outline, a story line, your characters, your plot, the arc of your narrative. You have to be with your writing through the good and the bad—just like a relationship. And you can't abandon it or feel that not being inspired or in flow says something about your writing or your talent. It doesn't. It just says that you're having a more challenging day. So you push through and do it anyway. Knowing that inspiration is only going to happen sometimes can help you become a more disciplined writer. Sometimes my best writing has come on nights when I didn't want to write. That in and of itself was surprising and rewarding. It reminded me of the value of just showing up. You never know what might happen—and in what myriad ways the divine might intercede in your writing life.

Platform Versus Passion

I work with two kinds of writers, and they exemplify two extremes: **the platform writer** and **the passion writer.** They're in fact not mutually exclusive, and I'd argue that the most successful writers are those who have figured out how to be both.

The platform writers are those of you who want to write a book to boost your credibility and professional legitimacy. You're an expert in your field, and you want a book for your clients, to bring in more business, to get speaking gigs. Most often these writers don't have a lot of time for their writing. They might even be "writing" a book aurally, hiring people to transcribe their work and then get it into book format. I work with several entrepreneurs who are doing just this—and it's a totally legitimate way to write a book. For these authors, their book is a product, and while they want it to look good and be something they're proud of, their identity isn't too wrapped up in the process or the publication itself.

Then there are the passion writers. You're a passion writer if you think about your book like it's your baby. If someone doesn't respond well to your work and you are crestfallen, you are a passion writer. You are doing the work that you love, and it's worked its way into the very core of who you are. This is a beautiful thing, but it comes with a price. Women often use pregnancy and laboring metaphors when they speak about their process, but far too frequently people who speak about their work like this are *too* attached to their projects and set themselves up to be devastated by the eventuality of the rejection and bad reviews that every single writer experiences at some point in their career.

It's not a bad thing to be a platform writer or a passion writer. However, if you're the former exclusively, you might want to adjust your strategy a little bit. I advise starting with a smaller product, an ebook or at least a short book, to get your feet wet. The problem I've seen platform writers get into is that they're so focused on their career and product that they later regret the ways in which they let other people take over their book, and sometimes lament not having written the book they wanted to write. They didn't connect enough to their passion and ended up putting out a product they couldn't be proud of in the long run. There are so many ways to bring content into the world, and each experience gets you closer to understanding the ways in which you are what you write. Make sure you're totally ready, and if you're going to hire someone to ghostwrite (again, a totally legitimate choice!), make sure you feel that the writing truly embodies and embraces who you are.

If you're all the way in the passion-writing camp, then you would benefit from taking a day off from your writing each week to focus on your platform. Publishing is changing so much, and it's harder than it's ever been to get published without a platform. Unfortunately, good writing doesn't make up for a nonexistent platform. You can build a platform, but it takes time. Working on your platform while you write is an important strategy for getting published. Also, importantly, never assume that your book is one of a kind. It's a beautiful thing to love your writing and be in love with the book you're writing. Yes, feel passionate about what you're doing, but be careful not to fall into the trap of feeling like a rejection of your book is a personal rejection of everything that you are.

Later down the road, it's an asset to have comparative titles—books that you feel are similar to yours, authors whose company you'd like to keep. It helps your agent and editor, too. That there are similar works out in the world need not be looked at as competition, but rather as contributing to a body of work that can always use new blood. And you can't be so tied to your words and your concept that you wouldn't change things when your agent or editor comes to you with feedback and editorial remarks.

I'm guessing that the vast majority of you probably relate a little bit to both the passion and the platform writer. Ultimately, find a healthy balance between the two. When you pitch yourself to an editor or agent, you want to be informed. You want to wow. The platform part tells the industry professional that you know what's up, that you're worth taking a risk on. (Because unless you have proven book sales from a previous book, you're a risk.) The passion part tells the industry professional that you're willing to kick your butt into high gear, that your book means the world to you, and that you'll do anything and everything it takes to see it through, promote it like crazy, and never ever lose your passion for and commitment to your project.

It's a hard act to balance—to be both. Neither extreme makes for an ideal publishing candidate, and being right in the middle is a lot to ask of yourself. So just feel into which is more true of you, and consider that you might need to focus your energy, your proposal, your attention on the other every once in a while—while you're writing, yes, but, more important, once you're ready to present yourself and your book to the world.

MINDSET CHALLENGE: ARE YOU OWNING YOUR WRITING?

Thinking of yourself as a writer is key to becoming and being a writer. Talking about yourself as a writer is critical to making your dreams and aspirations around publishing a reality. We will talk about platform in Chapter 4, but if you are currently writing in obscurity and no one knows you're writing a book, and you're not talking about it with anyone, what do you think is going to happen when you're ready either to shop to an agent or a publisher or to self-publish your book? That's right. There will be no readers!

I'm a big fan of living out loud with your writing. If you struggle to talk about what you do with friends and family, you need to start there. Talk to people about what you're writing. Tell people you're writing a book. It's a built-in accountability structure, too. Yes, it's painful when people ask you about your book and you have to tell them that you're not making progress, but it will also remind you that you said you wanted to write that thing in the first place.

I decided to go onto YouTube with my own announcement that I was going to write a book. I did this specifically because I knew being public with my intention to write would make me get it done. There is no way this book would have been finished in the time it took me to write it if I hadn't made this rather brazen and bold declaration that I would complete my book in six months—a deadline I felt I had to make or else. This was about doing my writing and having an accountability structure, but it was also about owning my writer self. As a writing coach, I often get asked about my own writing. For years I said I was content not to write a book, until all of a sudden I realized I really needed to—and I had something to say. This was a big shift in my consciousness about who I was. It was about owning the writer in me whom I'd denied. I'd somehow convinced myself that working with writers was enough. I didn't need to write or publish because I was working with authors every single day. Shifting my scope—widening my own understanding that I could do both, work with authors and write—helped me to own my writing. And I'm grateful for this shift.

How about you? Do you currently own your writing? Do you talk about your writing with your family and friends? With strangers? In what ways are you disowning your writing, and why? If you totally own it, what are the ways in which you do this? It's as important here to identify how you aren't owning your writing as it is to acknowledge yourself for all the ways in which you do. If you're doing it every day, you deserve a big cheer, and if you need a little work in this area, start by introducing yourself to me as a writer. I'm serious—visit me on Facebook and say, "Hello, I'm so-and-so and I'm a writer." I welcome you to test this out with me in a public space and see how it feels.

The Pain of Procrastination

Procrastination is one of those ubiquitous beasts that impacts a lot of writers, and it stems from disowning. When we aren't writing, we aren't owning our writing. It's as simple as that. What's not as simple are all the reasons for not writing. It may be because you are stuck. It may be because you don't have the time. It may be because you're prioritizing other things over your writing. But whatever it is, your procrastination is a very big sign showing you the ways in which you're not owning your writing. So look deeply into this particular behavior and see what you want to do to make a change.

We all procrastinate. It's human nature. Some people even work well on a tight deadline, procrastinating as a means to create pressure for themselves. If you have a poor relationship with time and deadlines and know your-self to be a procrastinator, then you also understand the ways in which it creates anxiety. There's nothing like not doing something to fan the flames of shoulding. Living with the idea that you *should* be writing every day is just another way to beat yourself up. And the more you think about writing and don't do it, the more you lose your sense of pride and ownership over your own writing. Consider this: If you've been procrastinating on your writing and someone who knows you're working on a book asks you about it, how do you generally respond? Sheepishly, right? *Oh yeah, I've just been putting that off.* Or, *Yes, the thing is that a lot is going on with me right now. I want to get back to it, but I'm not sure when. Soon, I hope.* These are the ways in which we backpedal, and we're thinking to ourselves, *I'm not really a writer. I haven't written in months. What am I doing?*

If this particular topic hits a nerve with you, let's work to challenge this mindset right here, right now. Say out loud: *I am a writer.* Go on. Say it. Especially if you're in a public place. All the better! Let it be your mantra. If this is easy for you, expand upon it. Make it as specific and interesting as possible. I had one client whose mantra was "I am a talented, hardworking mystery writer who is strong, courageous, and devoted to my work." Every time she sat down to write, she repeated this to herself, and I'm sure I don't need to tell you how inspiring it was for her. It changed the way she approached her writing, and it legitimized her efforts toward becoming a genre writer and finishing her mystery novel. If you've never been big on mantras, challenge yourself again. Try it on. *You are a writer.*

MINDSET CHALLENGE: IS PERFECTIONISM GETTING IN YOUR WAY?

Where do we get it into our heads that we can't show anyone our work until it's perfect? Many writers suffer from this misconception, and it results in their toiling away in isolation with their projects, never showing anyone their work, never getting feedback, and effectively creating a bubble of an existence around their writing. The irony here, of course, is that your work is going to be much less than perfect if you've never opened yourself up to feedback and constructive criticism. Fear of criticism may well be a reason people don't show their work in the first place, but writing that's done in a bubble has no oxygen. If you want to become an author and get published, it's time to start showing your work—on a blog, in a writing group, with a friend, and to a professional. Your work is your art, created for the purposes of being read. Just as we'd find it sad for beautiful artwork to be covered up by tarps in an attic, so too is it sad for beautiful works of writing to be stored in file folders, buried in your computer for no one to see. Let it out. Give it air and light and life.

The question of whether your work is ready to show is something you need to feel into. Some of you suffering from crises of confidence may have no idea how good your writing really is. And even if it needs a lot of work, that doesn't qualify it as bad. In her book *Bird by Bird,* Anne Lamott coined "shitty first draft," a term I love for its permission to create crap! We all need this permission in our writing. Very few of us are capable of churning out perfect manuscripts on the first go-around, and oftentimes with my clients, the most important thing we're doing is drawing out the story. Writing is a process, and messiness is key. If you can't allow yourself to ever be messy, you might not ever find out where your creative mind wants to go. You may be self-editing so much that you're stifling your characters and your own creativity. The primary takeaway here around perfection is that it's unattainable. And in striving for something unattainable, you're setting yourself up for suffering.

The Power of Perspective

Whenever one of my clients gets stuck, they're treated to a perspective exercise, which is all about identifying where they're at with their writing and where they might go. The power of perspective is made all the more clear when we can feel into how truly miserable and debilitating our current perspective really is. I have had clients describe their current perspective on their writing as vacant, cold, claustrophobic, devoid of color, miserable. If this were a landscape, would you be inspired to write?

Allowing yourself to feel into other perspectives that exist if and when you're feeling stuck in a low-energy or paralyzing place with your writing can really loosen things up. One of my clients, a self-proclaimed perfectionist, identified "dessert first" as a perspective she wanted to try for a few weeks. So for one month, every time she came to her writing, it was with this orientation toward dessert first. For her, this was playful and fun. It meant she wasn't going to approach her work as "hard," something that had been holding her back. It meant she was going to give herself permission to play. Maybe she'd take her computer outside with her, or have a beer on the patio, or play some fun music in the background, while she wrote. It was a way of shaking up the seriousness she'd brought to her writing life, when she wasn't even sure where she'd picked it up and why she was embodying it.

The perfectionists among you need permission to play. Think of something that brings you joy—an animal, a flower, a kind of food, a landscape, a destination—and try bringing some of the aspects of that thing or place to your writing. If it's the ocean, for instance, put images of water around your writing space and play ocean sounds while you write. If it's an animal, like a dog, think about how a dog might approach a writing assignment, and give yourself a couple of minutes to settle into that sense of carefree-ness or happy-go-lucky-ness that's possible for you with your writing. This is about shaking things up, and particularly about freeing yourself from the idea that your writing needs to look any particular way. You might truly surprise yourself by reconnecting with your writing in a way you haven't felt in years. Even if you've been quite prolific, it's possible that you approach your writing from the standpoint of "it has to be perfect" or "it's hard work." It's a pretty common stance. Only you have the power to try on something new. Give it a try, even if it feels embarrassing. You have nothing to lose.

Simplify

Another affliction of some perfectionists is the belief that things aren't supposed to be or allowed to be simple. Perfectionists tend to complicate and overthink. They're their own worst critics, of course, and the idea that other people might criticize their work will send them right back into that writing bubble even if they've had the courage to emerge on a few occasions.

I've found that perfection, in its unattainability, makes writing harder and more complex than it needs to be. Trusting your own voice is a practice, but it's also something that can and will change the way you write. Some writers are trying so hard to be something they strive to be. They're trying to emulate an author they admire, or reach the bar they've set for themselves about what qualifies as "good" writing. If you are a naturally talented writer, that's one thing, but the vast majority of writers have to work on their craft for years and years to become masters. Novice writers who believe that they should be like Toni Morrison, Ian McEwan, Jonathan Franzen, Barbara Kingsolver, or Ann Patchett right out of the gate not only set themselves up for disappointment but also don't give themselves permission to find their own voice.

I can offer a straightforward solution here: simplification. Yes, simplify your style. Try writing short sentences. Try writing a simple scene with two characters about something cliché. Write your narrative like you talk. Share a scene from childhood in the voice of the girl or boy you once were. Tell your prospective reader something about yourself as if that person were your best friend and you were sitting down at a bar to dish. These kinds of writing prompts allow you to explore the kind of writer you really are, rather than the kind of writer you think you're supposed to be.

Many writers hung up on perfect get stuck because their sentences have to be perfect. But again, there is no perfect, and even if you believe there are examples of it in the literary world, how often do you think a perfect novel or a perfect memoir is written? Popular novels and memoirs often capture a particular voice, experience, or energy that's interesting because it's unique, experimental, of its era, or of its region. Be you. Bring your unique experience and way of thinking to your work. Don't try to stifle or change who you are in order to make your writing more palatable, more literary, or even more commercial.

My advice here to simplify has to do with becoming you. You know how it is in high school when kids try on a bunch of different identities to try to figure out where they fit in? It can be the same with writing. We can try and try, without realizing that who we are as writers really stems from our essence. If you're putting too much effort into being a certain kind of writer or to make your work fit a certain style, I urge you to take a step back and start from the beginning. I urge you to hit the reset button and start with what you know. I often use David Whyte's beautiful poem "Start Close In" with my clients when they start spinning out and losing their centeredness. Its opening stanza— *Start close in / don't take the second step / or the third / start with the first / close in / the step / you don't want to take*—is a wonderful and inviting challenge to leave all that other stuff behind. In starting close in, you start with what you know. You claim your own story, your own voice, and sometimes even the exiled writer inside of you who is longing to come home.

I Am Shit and I Am Special —Two Sides of the Same Sticky Coin

For some people, the very idea that anyone can write a book sets off red flags. *If everyone can write, then how can I be special?* Or, *That's not true. Not everyone can write, and here's a list of crappy published books to prove my point.*

This mindset illustrates a place where writers get stuck. Believing you are special, ironically, can be as paralyzing as believing you are shit. As hard as it might be to acknowledge, it's the flip side of the same coin. The writer who believes they aren't good enough gets mired down in old messages from parents, teachers, anyone who told them to get real or who criticized their writing. The special ones among you might have had your creative pursuits fostered by family and mentors. Or maybe you've overcome hurdles and worked hard to get to a place of truly knowing you're a good writer. But the messages are still strong. You have to produce, be the best, get published on a big house, get a big advance, keep writing, keep being better. In both scenarios, the pressure-cooker we create for ourselves can be detrimental to our writing.

If you're lucky, you're somewhere in the middle of this spectrum. You haven't been criticized to the point of feeling like you can't or shouldn't write. Or, if you have, you've had enough healing around it that you're now pushing forward. You aren't so blinded by illusions of grandeur that you can't see that there's room for improvement. You understand that you have to work to get published. It's true that there are a lot of bad books out there, but rather than letting this hold you back, you feel motivated. *I can get a book published, too!*

Rank yourself on a scale from 1 to 10, 1 being the *I'm not good enough* place, 10 being the *I'm better than everyone else* place. You don't have to share your number with anyone. It doesn't matter to anyone except you. And your number won't determine your future successes, either.

There are plenty of published and successful 1's, and there are many 10's who overcome their need to measure up. If you're already smack-dab in the middle, then you have a leg up. You're a writer who doesn't suffer from crises of confidence or envy. For the 1's, just calling yourself a writer is a first important step toward being a writer. For the 10's, becoming an author is about legitimacy and external validation (which we'll get into in more detail directly below), and any rejections and delays are going to feel intense and crippling. And yet you need to own your writing just as much as the 1's.

Everyone notice what comes up when you say the mantra I encouraged you to try on earlier: *I am a writer.* If you feel so inclined, write down your thoughts. Record your memories, impressions, associations, judgments, ambitions.

MINDSET CHALLENGE: HOW MUCH IS EXTERNAL VALIDATION FUELING YOU?

What motivates you to write? Is it your passion for the craft, the tingling feeling of articulating what you want to say in just the right way? If you close your eyes and think about it, most of you can probably come up with some pretty powerful motivators, things you love about writing that keep you striving and continuing to write, even when it gets hard.

Connecting to this feeling is a good place to start all of your writing sessions, because what's coming next is a struggle for most writers: What motivates you to keep going, finish, or follow through with your writing goals? Writing just to write is one thing. It's a wonderful pastime, and it can make you feel good, sure. But writing with an end goal in mind is a whole other game. I work with people who have an end goal in mind—even if that's just finishing a memoir that they want to share only with their family. I'm interested in helping writers get published, yes, but I'm more interested in getting writers oriented toward completing a project—whether that's a series of essays, a novel, a memoir, or a how-to book. We're talking big projects here.

You know the difference between writing to write and writing to publish, I'm sure, and while writing just to write holds almost no tension, writing to publish holds quite a lot. Writers who have written for years in bliss, moving along and stashing little pieces away here and there, suddenly hit a wall when it comes to working on a book, especially if they hope to get it picked up by an agent or sell it to a publisher. This hitting the wall has to do with moving from a place of being very self-motivated (often because there's less discipline involved in writing just to write) to being driven by outside forces. Once you decide you want to publish, not only are you letting the outside in, you need that to happen in order to get published. Suddenly, someone else holds the key to what happens with your writing. As soon as you decide you want to publish, a whole host of questions opens up about how that's going to happen. And if you want to get an agent and publish on a traditional house, all of a sudden, you open yourself up to the eventuality that you will have to be accepted or rejected.

As soon as you decide you want to publish, what happens out there in the world of publishing starts to influence your writing. I think this is a good thing when it comes to schedules and discipline, but it can be a very bad thing when it comes to our emotions. I've seen too many authors put all their eggs into the baskets of various publishing folks only to have their writing dreams killed. Preventing this from happening is key to your survival as a writer, and it's why it's important to check this mindset. If you are a person who's hinging your worth and merit as a writer on whether an agent or an editor accepts your work, you need to press the reset button. You might not find out that this is true until you get your first rejection from someone you really hoped would represent you. If and when that happens, come back for the pep talk that follows.

Have a Plan—and a Backup Plan

It's great to want to be published on a traditional house. This is the dream of most writers who seek to be published—to find representation by an agent and to be picked up by a publisher. And it's a solid plan A. But it should not be your only plan. I advise having a plan, and then at least one, if not two, backup plans.

Depending on your publishing goals, a good plan A is to seek representation by an agent, who will then (hopefully) sell your book to a publisher. For those of you wanting to publish on a big house, this is definitely plan A, as you cannot approach big publishers without an agent. Any unagented project that's submitted to a publishing house is considered "unsolicited," and while there are many houses that do accept unsolicited projects, most of the big houses do not. End of story. If you are not agented, you are not invited to submit. Once you're agented, your agent will shop your book around to various editors. Depending on the agent's strategy and hope for getting picked up, he or she will shop it either exclusively, to a few houses, or widely. Many agents shop books to many, many houses, working tirelessly for their clients until they sell or do not sell the book. While many of you will get picked up by an agent who will sell your work, some of you will get agented only to have your work not be sold. This is disappointing. Writers put a lot of weight on being agented, as if this guarantees getting published, but of course it does not. The fact that many agented manuscripts do not sell is another reason to have a backup plan.

Plan B is for any writer who cannot get an agent to pick up their work, or for any writer who was agented but couldn't get a bite from a publisher. Plan B is selling your work directly to a publisher, without representation. The course of action is the same as shopping to an agent. You send query letters and sample writing or proposals, except these letters are addressed to editors rather than agents. You cannot send your work to the big houses, true, but there are plenty of small presses that accept unagented work. And you want to do your homework. Find out the name of the editor you're pitching to, and make sure that your book is a good fit for the list you're trying to sell your work to. It's not worth your time or any editor's to do a blanket submission process. I can't tell you how many times, as an acquiring editor, I received submissions from writers cc'ing a ton of other editors in the same email. Big mistake. I would never write those people back. You must tailor your letters to the particular editor and the house you're pitching to.

If, after trying for an agent and an editor, you don't succeed, plan C, in my opinion, is self-publishing. For some of you, self-publishing is going to be plan A. I am self-publishing this book, and knew I was doing so from the get-go, so no need for a backup plan. But knowing that self-publishing is a backup plan if you're aspiring to publish traditionally is a good thing, because it helps you know what you have invested in your project. If you can't sell it, will you give up on the project and let it sit in a file on your computer to be killed when your computer dies, or to be found by your kids or grandkids after you pass? I know, this probably sounds morbid, but you need to ask yourself what you want to happen to this book project that you're investing so much of your time, energy, and passion into if you can't sell it.

Any time I work with a new client, I ask them about self-publishing. If they can't sell their book project, will they self-publish? I want to know because it helps me gauge how much having the work out in the world matters to them, versus having the work published by a particular house. For me, this says something about how much value you're placing on being approved. Yes, you can want this all to unfold a certain way, but if it doesn't, then what? Will you pursue your publishing dreams no matter what? It's a valuable thing to know because it lessens the pressure you put on yourself to be "accepted" by agents and editors. It can help you write your book for you and your readers as you go, rather than for agents and editors. I always encourage my writers to envision the friendly faces of their readers as they write their books. Knowing whom you're writing for can provide a lot of motivation. If you're inadvertently writing for the agent or editor who will hopefully accept your work, you're not writing for the right people.

Become Your Own Gatekeeper

Agents and editors are known as the industry gatekeepers because they're the ones, as we've been discussing, who get to decide what gets published and what doesn't—when it comes to traditional publishing. I'm not suggesting here that everyone opt to self-publish. Not at all. But I am suggesting that you don't give agents and editors so much power.

Finding an agent or an editor is a lot like dating. It has to be a good match. They have to really love your book and what you have to offer, or they don't want to represent you. It can be hard not to take this personally, and yet do you really want to "be" with someone who doesn't absolutely love what you have to offer? Do you want representation from someone with whom your work doesn't absolutely resonate? Of course not. Think of your pursuit of an agent or editor like this: Not everyone is going to be the right fit, and this doesn't mean that your work isn't valuable.

Oftentimes agents and editors reject manuscripts and proposals simply because an author's platform isn't strong enough. We'll be talking about this a lot more in Chapter 4, but it's good to understand why you're getting rejected and what you want to do about it. Getting published is not supposed to be easy. The barriers are high because publishers risk a lot to put books out into the world—especially because most books don't earn out their advances, and most books don't sell what they need to sell to make the publisher a profit. It's a business decision for agents and editors; it's not a personal assessment of why you are good or bad.

Becoming your own gatekeeper means knowing the intrinsic value of what you have to offer. You become your own gatekeeper when you self-publish, for sure. I love writing this book knowing that my readers are going to get value out of it, and knowing that I don't have to worry about an editor changing my words or whether my publisher is going to be pleased with the results of my sales. I trust that my own copyeditor will tell me what to change, and my expectations for sales are fairly modest: I want to earn back what I've put in. And with that, I will be happy. And I can tell you this: Being my own gatekeeper feels damned good. I'm not worrying about whether this book will pass some sort of litmus test. I already know my platform isn't big enough to garner me a huge advance on a big publishing house. So I'll keep working on it, and for now this book is out in the world and it's something I can be proud of.

Assess Your Tolerance for Rejection

This is a big one. Know that the vast majority of you will experience rejection from an agent or a publishing house, or both. If you already know you struggle with rejection, you need to mentally prepare yourself. I would start by placing affirmations all around you the moment you start shopping your work. Remind yourself that your work is good and valid. Remind yourself of the kind of writer you are or aspire to be.

As a preventative measure that's less about building up your emotional reserves, I also strongly recommend that you get an editorial assessment of your work. This can be an assessment of your entire manuscript, or of your proposal. But having a pair of professional eyes on your work can at least prepare you for what you might hear from an agent or editor.

But once you've done that and feel you are ready to show your work to the world, know that you will be let down. This can feel crushing, or it can serve as motivation. I recommend asking an agent or editor for more details about why you are being rejected, for the purpose of information gathering. Some writers feel embarrassed to do this, but I always ask: What do you have to lose? If an agent or editor will share more details about their decision making, this arms you with the knowledge you need to make changes in your proposal or your manuscript. It might send you back to the drawing board, or it might help you reassess how much time you're putting into your social networking. Whatever the case may be, if you can muster up the courage to do it, ask.

And consider this. Many famous authors have wonderful rejection stories to tell. Augusten Burroughs was rejected countless times before his memoir *Running with Scissors* went on to become a national bestseller. I recently had coffee with Julia Scheeres, author of *Jesus Land* (a brilliant memoir), and she told me that her agent had all but given up on her manuscript when she happened to sit down with an editor who shared a fundamentalist background similar to Julia's. Remember what I said about the process of shopping a book being like dating: When a book resonates with an agent or an editor is when it sells. And sometimes you can actually pinpoint editors' and agents' interests and try to hook them with a particular detail of your book. In the dating world, this might be called stalking, but in the publishing world, it's called thorough research. Don't be afraid to go there!

MINDSET CHALLENGE: ARE YOU LIVING LIKE AN AUTHOR IN YOUR EVERYDAY LIFE?

Living like an author means making the time to *be* an author—to write, yes, but also to lay the groundwork for taking yourself seriously as a writer. You do this by claiming it with your family and friends, as we've discussed above in the sections on valuing and owning your writing. But it also takes self-identifying as an author, and embodying this idea of being an author when people ask you what you do. It's got to infiltrate your life in every way.

Reminding yourself to think, act, and live like a writer

until you don't have to remind yourself anymore will change the way you think about yourself, the way you approach your writing, and even how you write. You can start to cultivate this mindset long before you become a published author. You've heard of faking it till you make it, right? This is one of my favorite pieces of advice, and there's no better place to employ it than in your writing. If you hang out with people who think that your writing is just a passing fancy, something you dabble in that's for fun, or cute, or just a pastime, you need to set them straight. You must let the people you care about know what your writing means to you, and what your goals and aspirations are. Our friends and family can be our biggest supporters, but not if they're taking their cues from us and we're doing a little dance around our writing that devalues it by (a) not making it a priority or (b) using language that discounts it. Remember, you set the tone for your own writing. If you take it seriously, others will take it seriously. If you make a commitment to live like an author, other people will start to take notice and they'll not only honor your choices but start to view you and talk about you as an author, too.

How Much of the Pie Does Your Writing Get?

I have a simple exercise I do with my authors who are struggling to complete their homework assignments, in which I ask them to create a pie chart of their priorities. The percentages represent the amount of time they give to the various commitments in their lives: work, family, etc., but also their various hobbies and habits: exercising; going on family outings on the weekends; meeting friends for dinner; watching TV; attending a cooking class. This can be as vague or as detailed as people want it to be, but it's all about time—because your time shows you where your priorities are. If I'm finding two hours a week to work on my book, that's a very small sliver of my pie, considering a week has 168 hours in it. And yes, sleep counts: fifty-six hours a week for those of us getting eight hours a night.

So do this exercise and take a look at what else in your life is getting more time than your writing. It may be that certain things—work, family, and sleep—are expectedly high. But what else is there? What else is on par with the amount of time you spend writing? Is talking on the phone with your mom or your kids rivaling the amount of time you spend writing? How about having dinner parties, or watching the latest series you can't get enough of? This is not a judgment. It's just about taking a look at the things that get as much time during your week as your writing does—or the things that get a lot more or a lot less. For me, there's no question that during the six months I was working on this book, I watched many more hours of old episodes of *The Wire* than I wrote. There came a point when I had to tell my partner that I wasn't going to watch the show every single time our family wanted to sit down and watch it. We were all hooked—no question—but I had to start opting out. Some nights this didn't happen, and you'd find me on the couch with everyone else, but other nights I decided that I needed to work a certain amount of time on my book each week in order to be able to claim that I was indeed a writer, an aspiring author, someone whose book really was going to be published.

How Do You Make the Time?

I've found that scheduling and accountability are the keys to making writing part of your everyday life. In order to publish, you have to dedicate time not only to your writing, but also to your platform. And while this doesn't have to be an everyday thing, it does need to be an every-week thing. I recommend posting to social media sites at least three times a week and blogging at least once a month. More on all of this is just pages away in Chapter 4, but for now, suffice it to say that you must make time every single day for some aspect of your writing.

Once you're an author, you will have a book or books out in the world that have a life of their own. If you want them to survive and thrive, you have to pay attention to them—just like children. You do not want to work your tail off to get published and then sit back and hope that other people will take care of your book, because that is not going to happen. No one, not even your publisher, is going to care about your book as much as you do. And this process of making sure your book has a good life starts now, before you're published.

So what does what I'm asking you to do really look like? How do you make the time? You start by blocking out your writing times. These should be in one-hour increments, at least. If you can write only three times a week, one hour a day, that's great. If you can fit in a little more, even better.

My favorite recommendation for people who are just getting started is the 3 x 3—three-hour blocks, three times a week. If you do this, you'll get nine hours of writing in every single week. You will be shocked by what you can get done in nine hours if you're not currently there already.

What next? There have to be consequences for breaking your dates with yourself. I highly recommend getting a coach or a writing partner who holds you accountable for your writing dates with yourself. You can set up a system whereby you check in with someone for each writing day, someone who is going to call you out on *not* doing what you said you were going to do, someone you have to report to.

The next big thing is enrolling your partner, friends, family, and even coworkers. Anyone who stands in the way of your keeping your writing dates must be enrolled. And it's not that they are intentionally trying to block you from writing! Far from it. These are the people who love you or want to spend time with you. They're your family out on the couch, wanting you to join them for an episode of your favorite sitcom. They're the colleague at work who wants you to come try the new restaurant down the street. They're the friend who spontaneously calls because she wants you to meet her at the bar in an hour. If you've made a commitment to your writing during these times, you have to be able to tell your family, your colleague, your friend what you're doing. Otherwise, how will they know? Only you know that you're breaking your date with yourself; no one else is any the wiser. Tell them what's up for you and ask for a rain check.

Finally, reward yourself when you do complete your goals. For me, my reward was posting on Facebook that I'd completed what I said I was going to complete. It didn't matter so much that people liked my post or that I got a bunch of virtual high fives. It was much more important to me that I treated Facebook as an accountability structure, and knowing that I could and would post my updates there and to YouTube helped me along. It was like having a virtual cheerleader. For some of you, more tangible rewards might work really well. You can take yourself out to dinner for every ten thousand words completed, or set up something really big for when you finish. Since I'm self-publishing, my big reward has always been about seeing my book in print by a certain date. Whatever works. But you gotta have a carrot.

Showing Up

Here is yet another term we use in relationships—*showing up*. Successful relationships are those in which people show up for one another. We are being good to ourselves if we show up for ourselves. Show up for your writing. Value it as you would any other truly important thing in your life. Not showing up for something you care about is grounds for going to therapy. So nip that one in the bud, too—and show up for your writing.

If you're simply not doing it, you need to take stock of why. If you're experiencing resistance around your writing, examine what's at the root. I've known writers who simply got off course, whose writing hung on them every single day for years, and yet they chose to do nothing about it. This is a bit like stopping exercising and knowing that you want to—should—go back to the gym but just not doing it. I've been there lots of times with my yoga, and the more time that goes by without going, the more I push out my return date. But then I go back and I think, *Geez, why didn't I come sooner?* Writing is a lot like this. It feeds us and motivates us, and showing up is often half the battle. If you can get yourself there, you will generally find that you have a worthwhile writing session.

Just getting yourself there can be hard when you're tired, busy, and prioritizing other things. I recommend visual support for those of you struggling to show up. Put Post-it notes in visible places as a reminder to show up to your writing. Place a big sign in your writing space that posts your word-count goals or your deadlines. I had a client who designated a stuffed animal she had as her writing muse. He lived in the living room of her apartment, but you could have something like this accompany you anywhere, reminding you to show up for your writing. I also recommend jewelry. Buy yourself a writing ring or a writing necklace. When you look at your hand or when you see your reflection in the mirror, it serves as a visual reminder of your commitment to your writing. These kinds of symbols are very powerful when they work, and if you're not showing up, you can employ as many of these exercises and structures as you need to change the tides.

MINDSET CHALLENGE: ONE THING AT A TIME

Each of the mindset challenges offered in this chapter is an opportunity to examine how you are serving your writing and yourself as a writer, and as the author you are or are going to be.

When it comes to certain ways of being and thinking about your writing, you may feel pretty secure that you're handling things well and that you're doing right by your writer self. In other ways, you might need to take a look at how you can help yourself to claim your writing as valuable, own your writing, let go of perfection, release the hold external validation has on you, or live more like an author in your everyday life. If you feel like you need to do more than one of these things, start with just one.

Remember that everything in this chapter is a practice, and practice makes habit—something that you just do. You can have a writing practice that becomes a writing habit, but you can also have a habit of valuing and owning your writing; a habit of writing from a place of internal motivation and inspiration; and a habit of prioritizing, scheduling, and showing up for your writing when you say you're going to. And if you break the habit, you hit the reset button and start fresh. It doesn't take a day or a week or even a month to build a new habit. It takes setting up triggers—structures—to remind you of what you say you want, and then it takes repetition.

Take the advice from this chapter that felt like something you could do. Maybe it's enrolling your partner.

Maybe it's buying yourself a necklace. Maybe it's emu-
lating something I described—like creating a mantra for
yourself, or putting it out there on YouTube or Facebook
that you're writing a book (include your deadline!). Ask
other writers how they value and own their writing, or
how they learned to write from a place of internal motivation rather than external validation (if you know this to be
true). Getting motivation and inspiration from community
is an important way to challenge your mindset. Finding a
place where you can share what's difficult and celebrate
your accomplishments is key to progress in the beginning. I encourage you to find these spaces—and they're all
over the place online. But find in-person or one-on-one
support, too.

Challenging your mindset is tough sometimes, but it's
also about challenging yourself to grow, become a better
writer, and do the things you say you want to do. This is
an important one, because writing can easily become that
thing you wish you were doing. And approaching it with
the right mindset can shift it from the thing you wish you
were doing to the thing you can't *not* do. Habit. Lifestyle.
You being a writer—an author—every single day, without
exception.

Chapter 4.
The Almighty Author Platform:
Understanding How and Why
to Build Your Platform So You Can
Prevent Rejections and Sell More Books

The reason a platform is called a platform is because of the visual image it suggests. According to *Merriam-Webster,* a platform is "a raised horizontal flat surface; *especially* : a raised flooring." It's also defined as "a place or opportunity for public discussion." When I think about platform, I often recall a scene from one of my all-time favorite movies, *The Life of Brian.* In this Monty Python classic, Brian steps up onto a platform above the crowd in order to escape detection by Roman foot soldiers. He figures he'll be safely ignored if he starts to preach from the platform because, as the viewer has already seen, the various other posts are occupied by bumbling fools whom no one's paying attention to. But Brian gets a small crowd of people gathered around him as he speaks; he says some things that make the group take notice. When he descends the platform because the foot soldiers have moved on, his little crowd follows him.

This scene depicts a perfect example of how creating a platform is not just about having a platform from which to speak. You can stand up in front of a crowd, but unless you have a message people want to hear, you may be completely ignored. Because what Brian says resonates with his listeners, he, in effect, develops a following. What works for him is the combination of getting up in front of people and having a message people want to hear. When it comes to creating an author platform, you need two things: to show up in a clear and consistent way, and to have good content. If you can do these two things right, the rest will fall into place. But it does require patience. A platform cannot be built in one week, or even one month. It's a slow build that takes being open to learning about what it entails, and time and investment.

WHAT IS AN AUTHOR PLATFORM?

Your author platform is anything that shows your future publisher that you have the potential to reach a wide readership. It is quantifiable by the numbers of people you have connections to—whether those are first-degree, second-degree, or even third-degree connections. When publishers talk about authors who have great platforms, they are generally referring to authors who have great websites and/or blogs (meaning interactive, functional, and with a clear and easy-to-find sign-up form); authors with a high number of followers across various social media platforms; authors with previous publications (of either books or articles); and authors who already have a fair amount of media exposure under their belts—through a list of public speaking engagements, YouTube videos showcasing their talents, radio links, TV footage, and/or a media packet. This type of platform is what authors have in place when they're securing six-figure advances. They are already go-to experts in their fields, and the numbers of followers they have are in the thousands.

Jessica Valenti, author of several books, including *Full Frontal Feminism* and *The Purity Myth* with Seal Press and, more recently, *Why Have Kids?* with Amazon's New Harvest, has twenty-two thousand Twitter followers and five thousand likes of her Facebook fan page as of this writing. Michael Hyatt, author of *Platform: Get Noticed in a Noisy World* (a book I read as research for this chapter) has 129,000 Twitter followers and 15,500 likes of his Facebook fan page as of this writing. Both of these authors have great platforms—national platforms. Jessica first came to Seal Press in 2006 as an author with a growing platform. Today she has all the components in place to make her a sought-after author. She's the go-to person on feminism, and she's established herself as an expert— perhaps *the* expert when it comes to her generation's feminism. Michael Hyatt, an expert on intentional leadership (and platform), has figured out a thing or two about how to get noticed. His book is way more comprehensive than this single chapter, and though it's about more than just books, I highly recommend you read it and follow his sound advice for getting noticed.

Publishers want authors who are regularly getting in front of crowds of people. Why? Because this sells books! Blogging, speaking, touring, and being active on social media are all part of the deal. Building an author platform is not for the shy writer who loves the solitude and quiet time offered by this particular form of creative expression. It's in fact the exact opposite. When you start to build your author platform, you will quickly realize that there is more to do than you can possibly take on. Unless you are a full-time writer, it's impossible to write a book and dedicate the kind of time required to have a platform the likes of someone like Michael Hyatt. But don't worry. You don't have to have 128,000 Twitter followers to catch a publisher's attention. You do, however, have to be tweeting.

WHERE DO YOU START?

Make an inventory of your online presence and your existing connections to people who would want to read your book—whether those are people you know or people you'd like to reach out to. Start by answering these questions:

- Do you have a website?
- Are you on Facebook, Twitter, LinkedIn, etc.?
- Are you connected to any organizations or "loudmouths" (people who like to spread the word about stuff) who could help you promote your book?

If you don't have a website and you're not on any social media, then it's likely that the whole idea of building a platform is going to feel overwhelming. Remember, you must start somewhere, and everything starts small. So the first thing you're going to do is get a website and sign up for Facebook and Twitter. Once you master these things, then you'll start adding more.

Your Website: Where Readers Come to You

When I first started Warner Coaching Inc. in 2004, I created my own website on Dreamweaver. I had my newsletter on Blogger and linked it to a tab on my site. As soon as I saw WordPress in action, I knew I had to migrate my site, but I was worried about the expense of it, and I held off until 2010. Now it's done, and it was worth every penny! If you haven't started a site yet, do yourself a favor and start up with WordPress. If you already have a site that's not a WordPress site, consider migrating it before you begin to expand it and add new features.

When you're first dreaming up what your website will be, decide whether you want it to be primarily a static site or primarily a blog. Static sites are for authors who want to have a home base and somewhere to direct their readers, but who don't want to post regularly, or update their content. These days, I recommend that authors have at least a blog function on their site, which is what my newsletter link is: WarnerCoaching.com/newsletter. I post only once a month, plus providing some sporadic updates here and there about things I'm working on. My site is not a blog, but rather a business site that I hope will get prospective clients to call me. However, that content I post once a month is a valuable part of my site, and something that keeps people coming back—even if it's not on a super-regular basis. I could post more often than I do, but at this point in my career, this is as often as I want to post, and the key is that I'm consistent. Once a month I write my newsletter. Readers know where to find it. And if they want to keep up to date on what I'm doing, they can subscribe to my newsletter and receive it as an email in their inbox once a month. The capacity for readers to sign up for my newsletter is another valuable feature I added to my site just recently for the sake of trying to capture names and email addresses of people who actively want to be in touch with me. Not having a sign-up form on your site is a lost opportunity to connect with your readers.

Tip: Easy-to-use email marketing systems include iContact (which is what I use); Constant Contact; MailChimp; and many others. Some are free, and some charge a monthly or yearly fee. It's easy to do a price comparison by Googling "email marketing systems." It's okay to start with a free system and upgrade once you have enough subscribers to merit moving to a bigger platform.

Social Media: Where You Reach Out and Engage with Your Readers

If you are not on Facebook or Twitter, set up those two accounts and worry about the other stuff later. Over time you can set up LinkedIn, Tumblr, Google+, Pinterest, and any others, but first get a consistent routine going with Facebook and Twitter. With Facebook, you have to have a personal account in order to set up a fan page, but the account you want to create for your author platform should be a fan page. You can call it your author page or your professional page, but the primary difference between your personal page and your fan page is that people don't have to friend you in order to follow your posts. When you get friend requests from people you don't know, you can direct them to "like" your author page. I do this a few times a week, just letting people know what's true—that I post pictures of my son only on my personal page, and all my good tips and information about writing and publishing are on my fan page at Facebook.com/warnercoaching.

Twitter seems to be a platform people either love or hate. I was resistant to it for a long, long time, until I realized how hugely important it is and how much I needed to be on it to grow my platform. Since I've taken the time to understand it better, I've found out how much fun it really is. The biggest reason for my resistance was one thing: time. I didn't want to be monitoring Twitter all the time. I find the Twitter feed to be incredibly overwhelming. When I refresh, sometimes five hundred or more new Tweets have been posted in a couple hours' time. However, I've now learned how to have conversations with people on Twitter. The game-changer for me was activating my phone so that I started getting texts any time someone mentioned me or wrote directly to me. Twitter is really not so different from texting, and once I wrapped my mind around that, I started tweeting every day.

Buy a simple Twitter how-to book, like *The Tao of Twitter*. This is a basic intro guide for businesses, but if you want to be a successful author, you need to start thinking of yourself as a business. As I said, you can tweet directly from your phone, just by texting a message to 40404. This posts whatever you text directly to your Twitter feed. You can have one-on-one conversations publicly or privately. You can join in on trends by following hashtags that cover topics of interest. All in all, you can be pretty engaged without feeling like you're getting too sucked in. But you have to give it a try.

THE TIME-SUCK REALITY CHECK

At this stage of the game, if you want to publish, the most important thing you have to offer up is your platform. How is that possible? you might ask. How can it be more important than my story, my writing, what I have to offer to my reader? The sobering truth is that it just is. If you have no online presence, no network of people to help you drive sales of your book, and no way to reach the potential readers of your book, publishers see that you are not ready to take on the challenge of marketing and promoting your own book. Similarly, if you self-publish, you will have no way to reach people who might want to read your book.

Consider yourself for a moment. How do you find out about books you really want to read? I'm sure some of you go to the bookstore and browse the stacks, but it's more likely than not that you've received a recommendation from someone you trust about a must-read book. It's very likely that this person heard about the book from either (1) a review, (2) a blog, or (3) a mailing. In order for your book to be mentioned in a review, a blog, or a mailing, you need to have connections and relationships. And you need to have enough rapport with an audience that people are going to be anticipating whatever it is that you're putting out into the world. Is this a lot to expect of yourself? Yes, probably. But if you believe that you will sell books, this is the mentality you must have. And how can anyone be anticipating what you have to say if you're not blogging, or if you're not active on social media?

So yes, it's important, and yes, it can be a time-suck. But it doesn't have to be if you learn how to manage your online commitments. The number one and best piece of advice I can give you is to start small. Do not jump in and start doing Facebook, Twitter, Pinterest, LinkedIn, YouTube, and Google+ all at the same time. Build over time. You can link your Facebook posts (from a fan page only) to post to your Twitter account. Do this. When you're first starting, post to Facebook once a day and to Twitter once a day. This way, because Facebook is linked to Twitter, you will be posting one Facebook post and two tweets per day. Limit these to Monday through Friday. Second, decide how often you want to blog. Once a month should be the minimum. I would recommend every other week for those of you really trying to build a platform. Then you can work up from there. Really successful and prolific bloggers generally blog three to five times each week, including some guest posts from other people to keep their traffic strong. This is unrealistic when you're first starting out, but you do want to assess your capacity for blogging and decide what you can do and stick to it.

All of this is time-consuming, but it doesn't have to take priority or precedence over your writing. Sit down and work out what your Facebook and Twitter posts are going to be on the weekend. Write ten Facebook posts and ten tweets. Use a program like HootSuite or Seesmic to load them up in advance so that you don't have to be logging on and posting every day. Once you start interacting with people on your Facebook and Twitter accounts, you'll again have to make some decisions about how you're using your time and energy. For some people, social media can become such an addiction that it detracts from their writing completely. I've known people who have basically stopped writing. Find ways to create a balance with it. I've never been an advocate for allowing social media to hijack your writing, and the most successful authors are those who have good boundaries. They turn off their Internet when they write. They develop a system that allows them to be engaged but not consumed. You want to figure out what system works for you and adhere to it until it becomes a habit.

AUTHOR BLOGGING 101

The first thing people start to worry about when they think about blogging or posting on Facebook and Twitter is what to say. Novelists especially tend to get worked up over this topic, and I've had more than a few try to convince me that they shouldn't be blogging or doing social media. But they've never won me over. There was a point in time when I believed you could still get a book deal without a website or a social media presence, but my sense is that this is no longer the case. I'm sure there are a few houses out there that will take the risk for the beauty of an author's writing or the power of their message, but if you're an unknown, why take that risk?

What's more important than what you write about on your blog, or what you post about on Facebook and Twitter, is what you shouldn't write about. Many authors make the mistake of thinking that posting a lot on any topic is building a platform. That couldn't be further from the truth. If you want to build a good author platform, you need to stay on topic and consistent with the themes of the book you are writing. If you are writing a book about the psychological benefits of sports, for instance, you want to be careful not to post too much about your other favorite pastime: home decorating. I see people doing this all the time. This stems from one of two misguided ways of thinking: (1) the author can't think of enough things to say about the topic they're writing a book about, or (2) the author is insistent on not getting pigeonholed into the topic they're writing a book about.

As I mentioned, both of these reasons for blogging about irrelevant topics are misguided because you are trying to establish yourself as a go-to person on one topic—not many topics. You don't want to dilute your message or confuse your audience. If you don't think you have enough to say about your topic, then you might want to revisit the way you're thinking about it. Some people get so focused in on a particular aspect of what they're writing about that they don't see the bigger picture. For instance, someone writing a memoir about being a Mormon doesn't need to limit their discussions to Mormonism. They could write about the way Mormonism is depicted in the popular culture, they could write about women and the Mormon religion, and they could write about religion at large.

For those of you worried about getting pigeonholed, I would argue that you're putting the cart before the horse.

If you don't have a following, if you're far from becoming the go-to person on the topic you're writing about, if you have just the bare beginnings of a platform—then you want to try to get noticed for one thing. You are diluting your message if you need people to see how dynamic and multidimensional you are by posting across topics and subjects that are seemingly disconnected (even though they might be connected to you). Memoirists most often feel scared about the ways in which their memoirs will say to the world, *This is all of who I am.* But again, first you need to get that memoir published. Once you've done that, you can start to worry about steering the train and what direction you want to be going in *next.* If you don't give your all to the project at hand first, you're not giving yourself the chance to deeply explore what you have to offer. Instead, you're so concerned with controlling how people see you that you're closing off opportunities to become known and seen for this one aspect of who you are—even if it doesn't represent the whole.

For those of us writing prescriptive books, it can seem a little easier to think of good posts. I subscribe to Google Alerts (Google.com/alerts) to keep track of various keywords and industry people so that I can follow what's happening and weigh in on the publishing conversation. I follow tons of people I admire on Twitter and try to read posts about things that are relevant to what I do. I'm also lucky because I'm in publishing and work with writers every day, so my own client sessions provide plenty of ideas for good posts. I have an app on my phone called Catch that I use to capture anything that I find inspiring or interesting, so that I never run out of ideas for my posts. I use a similar method for capturing Facebook and Twitter, and I also repurpose content from old newsletters. This makes good sense because my blog is five years old, but viewers can access only two years' worth of content. If you have old stuff, as long as it's still relevant, you want to be thinking about ways to repurpose—especially for social media sites where posts are supposed to be very short, such as Twitter, which is limited to 140 characters.

But what if you're writing memoir or fiction? What do you do? First of all, do not fall into the woe-is-me quicksand, where there's no possible room for the expansion of your inner creative genius, who knows that there is plenty to say about your topic. Most important, do not blog about things that have nothing to do with your book. When you do this, you're losing readers—except for your family and friends, who care about everything you do.

If you are a writer who wants to get published, your blog is not a place to practice being a better writer. It's not a place to tell people what you're thinking about today, or to share a story about your kids (unless you're writing a book about your kids). I often tell my clients to imagine that they're wearing a particular pair of glasses when they blog. The lenses comprise the themes that run through their book. Being an author blogger is all about focus. If you're writing a travel memoir, for instance, your blog needs to be about traveling. I have rejected manuscripts before based on the fact that an author's blog has nothing to do with their topic. Maybe once upon a time this travel author had a travel blog, but then the trip ended and there was no more travel going on. So the blog turned into one about all the things she loves about living in New York City and the foods she likes to eat. As soon as an editor sees this, they will be confused. And that travel writer has likely just lost her shot at a book deal.

So what should this travel writer have done? She could have continued to write about traveling—about other people traveling or her love of traveling or missing traveling. She could have written posts about her time abroad and stories that, even though they're not at the forefront of her daily experience, have to do with her book. She could have posted short little excerpts from her memoir, maybe a line or two that would have served as a lead-in to blog about travel in a thematic, rather than a specific, way. If she had done these things, an editor might have gone to her blog and found something cohesive. Something that made sense. Something that would have shown that this author really wanted to be a travel writer.

And novelists need to be thinking in the exact same way, and wearing that same pair of glasses. What is your book about? Are you writing a novel about American politics? A novel about a woman who gets revenge after her husband leaves her for a younger women? A novel about a twentieth-century American farmer who loses his farm due to social and cultural changes? All of these examples pose amazing opportunities for educating readers. American politics is easy. If your protagonist is someone within the administration, for instance, you can blog about the real-life people who have these jobs. You can also write about history, about events that have shaped our country and our people, and about anything else that's a through-thread in your own book. What about the woman who gets revenge? You can blog about real-life examples of that, too. You can set up Google Alerts to notify you if there's ever anything in the news about "divorce" + "revenge." When I was writing this book, Christie Brinkley was all over the news, as she was going through a very public and ugly divorce with her ex-hus-band Peter Cook. If your novel features characters who are having experiences similar to those of real-life people, this kind of story is up for grabs. It can also catapult your readership, because all of a sudden you are writing about newsworthy topics and tying them back to your blog. If one of your posts goes viral, you can go from having one hundred readers to having thousands of readers over-night, which is what every blogger is hoping for.

Another thing you can do as a memoirist or novelist is write about your writing process. Share things you're learn-ing, mistakes you've made, and ways in which you carve out time to write. You can also interview other writers and feature those interviews on your site. You can review other books and write about what you loved and didn't love so much. There are countless ways to keep a blog up to date and, more important, relevant. While these sugges-tions are some ways to get you started or keep you going, I would also recommend visiting the sites of other writers you admire. See what they're doing and how they're doing it and emulate!

If you're reading this and feel worried that you've been going about blogging or social media the "wrong" way, don't fret. It's not too late to change course, and it doesn't mean you need to delete your old posts. Just set your sights on the subject matter at hand and put on those theme-colored glasses every time you sit down to blog or to compose a Facebook or Twitter post. Sketch out a bunch of ideas. Use Catch to capture thoughts that occur to you when you're going about your day. Set yourself up for success!

HOW TO SHOWCASE YOUR PLATFORM IN YOUR BOOK PROPOSAL

Your platform is going to show up all over your book proposal in subtle and overt ways. To recap the elements of a nonfiction book proposal, they are: pitch letter, overview, author biography, comparative titles, target audience, marketing/publicity, and, finally, chapter-by-chapter summaries, and sample chapters. The only sections where you won't include anything about platform are, in fact, these last two sections, which are oriented exclusively toward your content.

Any opportunity you have to toot your own horn in a proposal, you do it. The book proposal is not a place to be shy or to downplay how amazing you are. Part of building your author platform is learning to think of yourself as someone amazing and fabulous and as someone who is worthy of having fans and followers.

In your **pitch letter,** you have two opportunities to showcase your author platform: in your opening, "hook" paragraph, and in your closing, about-you paragraph. If there's something unique you can share about yourself in that opening graph, do it. For instance, I've had clients who run their own schools with hundreds of students. A hook graph might lead with something like, "At the Prestige School, where I've served as the founder and CEO for the past five years, my students often talk about how the concepts I teach have opened their eyes to a new way of understanding business. Of the three hundred students who've gone through my program, 245 of them have gone on to found their own businesses." Does this sound arrogant to you? Perhaps. But does it also sound impressive? Would you want to know more about this Prestige School, and would the author have gotten your attention? She certainly got mine.

In your closing graph, you want to make sure to talk about your following—whether that's the number of people on your mailing list, the number of people you impact through your work, or your social media following—but only if you have a wide reach. If you don't, it's better just to showcase your primary strengths and what makes you the best candidate to write the book you're writing. Finally, no matter how small, if you have previous publications, they belong in the pitch letter.

In your **overview,** you also want to look for ways to mention what you do. For instance, I might refer to my coaching or my clients several times without needing to restate that I'm a coach. If you're writing a book about showing dogs professionally, you want to talk about awards you've won. If you race sailboats, mention races you've participated in and any accolades you've received. If you're writing on a topic that's more universal, talk about ways in which you're involved with particular communities of like-minded or similarly impacted people. For instance, if you're writing a memoir about going through a divorce, or being the child of gay parents, or surviving anorexia, talk about the organizations you might be involved with that deal with those issues. This is showcasing your connections, and it will be repeated in the **marketing/publicity** section, but don't be afraid of repetition! Another thing to focus on is your inspiration for writing the book in the first place. If you're writing a prescriptive book, is it going to inspire people, help people, add something that's missing to the current literature? If you're writing memoir or fiction, get personal. What about your personal experience prompted you to want to write the book? If it's fiction, don't feel afraid to share what parts of the book are "true." While not platform-related, per se, this kind of divulging helps explain why you're the person to write this book, and it can showcase how your passion (by way of experience) will propel you toward reaching your readers.

In the **target audience** and **comparative titles** section of your proposal (nonfiction only), you have another opportunity to talk about platform. In **target audience,** you want to restate the numbers of people you can reach. Give statistics of the number of people impacted by whatever you're writing about. If you're writing a memoir about a parent failing from Alzheimer's, don't forget to include how many people suffer from Alzheimer's, and how many children of ailing parents find themselves coping with this kind of situation. If you've written any guest posts on your topic for another blog, put that blog in the target audience section, along with any other blog, magazine, or outlet that might help you reach your readership. In the **comparative titles** section, you want to describe, in one paragraph, how your book is similar to and different from the title you listed as comparative/competitive/complementary (they're all the same). Use this opportunity to restate (remember, repetition is the name of the game) anything about your platform that might be relevant. For instance, maybe you've written a cookbook for parents that's focused on improving unhealthy diets and poor cooking habits, and because you're a youngish, attractive guy, people always compare you to Jamie Oliver. You want to use that to your advantage but also showcase how you're different. Here in the **comparative titles** section, in the paragraph in which you're talking about Jamie Oliver's book, you would want to restate something you've surely already included in your overview and marketing sections, which is that that your *Cooking at Home with Dad* series reaches a subset of the market that Oliver's does not, and then give statistics (yes, again) on how many stay-at-home dads there currently are in the United States.

The **marketing/publicity** section of your proposal is where you get to go wild with platform data. This section exists as a marketing tool, and its sole purpose is to make a case to your would-be agent or editor that you understand how to reach your readers. This is not the place to make a case for the fact that there's an audience. You already did that in the **target audience** section. This is the place to talk about where your readers hang out. It's the place to make long lists of TV shows, radio stations, and magazines that might want to feature your work. If you have connections to any of these media outlets, that's wonderful, but it's not required. The point of this section is to show the person reading the proposal that you understand that you have to cast your net wide and that you've uncovered any and all stones in your efforts to understand who your readers are, what they like, and where they spend time.

The primary tools to use for the purpose of weaving into the **marketing/publicity** section information that's both impressive and helpful to your would-be agent or editor include:

1. Statistics: Use statistics wherever possible to talk about your target demographic. Remember, it's important to differentiate your **marketing/publicity** section from your **target audience** section. Here you're using stats to say things like, "14% of family caregivers care for a special needs child—an estimated 16.8 million care for special needs children under 18 years old (National Alliance for Caregiving/AARP, 2009)" or, "According to a 2005 article by Pew Internet & American Life Project, some 55% of adult Internet users have looked for 'how-to,' 'do-it-yourself,' or repair information online, and roughly 1 in 20 Internet users—about 7 million people—search for repair help on a typical day." These are called "marketing points" in the industry because they make the case that real numbers exist to support your claim that there are people out there who will want to read your book.

2. Lists: Compile lists of TV shows, radio shows, and magazines, but this also includes organizations, blogs, and ezines. Use any and all of these outlets as subheads in your **marketing/publicity** section to make an impression. If I were writing a spiritual memoir, for example, I might include a subsection that reads something like this:

> Women's interest magazines regularly cover stories about women's personal journeys. Warner's story will appeal to mainstream readers of the following magazines:
>
> *Ladies' Home Journal*
>
> *Self*
>
> *Ms. magazine*
>
> *Woman's Day*
>
> *Redbook*
>
> *O, The Oprah Magazine*
>
> *Women Today*

You might wonder about the point of including this kind of research in your proposal, but remember, your proposal is a marketing tool—and it should never be seen as anything other than that. Agents and editors need all the ammunition they can get to make a case for your book. Agents are selling to editors, and editors are selling to their editorial boards and ultimately to the reps who in turn sell your book to book buyers who sell your book to consumers. The more robust your **marketing/publicity** section, the better equipped your agent or editor will be to make the case that you're worth taking a risk on.

3. Your personal marketing plans and/or connections:

You want and need to drive home all ideas, plans, connections, and favors you might be able and/or willing to pull. This may include possible speaking engagements, even if they're not yet booked. You could say you'll approach your local JCC, for instance, even if they haven't formally invited you to speak. As long as it's true, you can say that you have a connection to Julia Roberts and that she may blurb your book. You don't necessarily have to deliver on all the things you propose, but you will need to try to make good on everything you say you're willing to do. Don't say you're going to start a blog, for instance, if you have no intention to do so, but do say that you'll blog every day if you're willing to, even if you're not currently doing so.

The **marketing/publicity** section of your book proposal is meant to show the ways in which you're thinking big—bigger than you might be feeling. It shows that you're thinking outside the box, and that when the time comes, you'll be a strong collaborator who's willing to take the initiative to help your publisher sell books. Publishers are relying increasingly on their authors to bring readers, and understanding this as you're creating your **marketing/publicity** section is key. You honestly can't go too big. And this is intimidating to a lot of folks. I've seen more than a few authors balk at the idea of having to sell themselves in this way. But trust me, it does pay off. Put in the time to create a solid presentation. Hire someone to do the research if you need to. Putting forward a flimsy **marketing/publicity** section (or proposal, for that matter) gives agents and editors a good reason to pass on your project. And giving it all you've got can make the difference between getting representation and a book deal and being left wondering why you got a rejection.

AUTHOR PLATFORM INVENTORY —THE WHAT'S WHAT

In an effort to walk you through the various aspects of platform that will get the attention of agents and editors, I'm proceeding here by listing the hot-button platform items, and how to use them or make headway toward making them work for you.

Before you dive in and get started, though, try this fun exercise. It's one I love and have written about often: Create an "I AM FABULOUS" list. This list will help you spruce up your author bio, but it will also serve as a reminder, something you can revisit when you get down in the dumps about your platform. Because, believe me, when you're first starting out, you're going to get down in the dumps from time to time. When you go on Twitter and see people who have thousands and thousands of followers, you're going to wonder how you'll ever rise to that level of notice. The truth is that maybe you won't, but you do need to put forth the effort, slowly and steadily, if you want to get published. This is true for traditional publishing and self-publishing alike. Don't think that platform doesn't matter for the self-published. It does, and maybe even more so. I've said this before in this book, but it bears repeating. No one is going to care more than you when your self-published book doesn't sell. True, you won't be letting your publisher down, but you will have invested your own time, passion, energy, and money into a project that just sits there. Platform is going to drive your sales, so you want to get on it sooner rather than later.

Your Website/Blog

Your website can be either static or interactive, and the biggest decision to make here has to do with where you want your blog feature to be. If it's on the homepage, that means you're really showcasing your blog and you want to update it often. Any daily blog you might visit (NYTimes. com, HuffingtonPost.com, Jezebel.com, DailyKos.com) is considered a blog site because it updates its content constantly and every time you check back there's something new. If you aren't going to blog more than once a week, you're better off just having a tab on your site, like I do with my newsletter (WarnerCoaching.com/newsletter).

The best URL you can have as an author is your name. Once you have a published book, it's a good idea to get the URL for your book as well, but in the beginning, just your name will do (e.g., BrookeWarner.com). You don't even want to buy the URL to your book title initially, because it's likely to change. I recommend using GoDaddy.com to purchase your URL. I also think they're a helpful company for beginners in general. Their hosting is good, and they will even walk you through how to install a WordPress theme.

The tabs you want to include on your site will include at least, but not be limited to, About; Blog; Read a Chapter; Contact. Depending on what you're writing about, you can include all sorts of other, more specific tabs, like

Inspiration; History of the Chesapeake; Resources; Important Links; My Story; Other Works; and more. Once you have a published book, you can add links like Reader's Guide; About the Book; Purchase the Book; My Publishing Journey; and/or Media.

Your website is also a place to interact with your readers, so make sure there's a contact tab. Mine is set up as a form (WarnerCoaching.com/contact) so that I don't have to post my email address on my site, which reduces the amount of spam I get. On my site I also have a tab called "Ask Brooke" (WarnerCoaching.com/ask-brooke). Consider something similar if you want to encourage your readers to interact with you. Giving readers an indication that you are there and ready to answer questions they might have can invite dialogue.

Make sure to add social media icons to your site as you grow your platform. You'll generally see at least Facebook, Twitter, and RSS feed icons on any given website, and these are all places that encourage people who land on your site to follow you in other ways.

Spend some serious time thinking about the layout of your site, and consult with a professional about how your content reads, whether you're sending a consistent message, and whether the energy you want to convey is coming across.

Note: There's a big difference between WordPress.com and WordPress.org. You do not want to go to WordPress.org unless you are planning to host your own site or build really big really quickly. The vast majority of authors will have more than enough power and functionality with WordPress.com, so stick with that in the beginning.

Social Media

Do what you can to make social media work for you without driving yourself crazy or letting it take over your life. Use HootSuite or Seesmic to load your content in advance. Start small and add on as you get a handle on what you're doing. Make sure to showcase your social media presence where you can. Add your links to the signature line of your email. Make sure to have social media icons on your website. Add Tweet and Like options to your blog to make it easy for your readers to share with others.

Facebook

Most people are on Facebook, which is why it's the number one social media site you want to focus your attention on initially. Some would argue that Twitter is more important and has a more accurate reach, but for authors, Facebook is still the place where you will have the most intimate access to your potential readership.

Create a fan page. Decide what it's going to be called. As long as you think you might write more than one book, you probably want to give it your own name. If you're writing a book that's connected to your business, like I am, then your fan page should be your business name.

Link your Facebook fan page to Twitter. This is easy to do by searching "help" inside Facebook once you have your account set up. The help function will walk you through how to link these things up.

Post at least once a day and probably not more than four or five times a day. Remember to provide good and relevant content. The rules of blogging apply to the rules of posting on your Facebook fan page. This is not your personal profile page, so keep on topic and keep your readers wanting more.

Twitter

It's possible that Twitter has surpassed Facebook in terms of its importance where general platform is concerned, but it is less intimate and more fact-driven, so I still think Facebook has an edge. Twitter allows you to post only 140 characters, so you have to be concise.

When you choose a username for Twitter, that is known as your handle. I chose @brooke_warner when I very first signed up for Facebook, and I'm glad I have it under my name rather than my business name because people are going to search for you by your name. Sadly, another Brooke Warner took @brookewarner. Your ideal Twitter handle is @yourname with no underscores or other characters.

The basics to know about Twitter are retweeting and hashtags. You can retweet other people's messages simply by hovering over anyone's tweet. The "retweet" link shows up and you hit it and voilà—there you go. The message automatically includes "RT," followed by the handle of the person whose message you're retweeting. You do this when you like what someone has written and you want to share it with your own followers. You may also choose to do this because you're following someone and you want to let them know that you like their post.

You want to keep in mind that other people may want to retweet your messages, too, so try to allow for enough space in your tweet for others to retweet it without cutting off the message. The way to do this is to calculate how many characters "RT" plus your handle total. Mine, "RT @brooke_warner" is 17 characters, so I need to make sure that any given message I hope will be retweeted in its entirety is no more than 123 characters.

My messages that are automatically linked from Facebook are generally longer than 140 characters, and Facebook includes a link so that if someone wants to link to the whole thing, they can. Some might insist that doing this is not the best Twitter etiquette, but at this point in time I still like having my Facebook page linked to Twitter.

Hashtags allow you to follow trends. Any time you put a hashtag in front of a word, you are tagging it so that anyone on Twitter can find it easily. Once you're on Twitter long enough, you will start to see popular hashtags. For writers, these are things like #amwriting, #writetip, and others. When you go to the link at the top of your Twitter profile page and hit "#Discover," you can type in anything you're interested in finding. If it's been marked with a hashtag, it will show up there, allowing you to follow trends you're interested in.

As I mentioned above, you can and should enable your phone to receive Twitter updates. You do this by going to Settings, and then to Mobile. Twitter will prompt you to type in your phone number, and then you can start Tweeting simply by texting your tweet to 40404. Very cool! If you're new to Twitter, feel free to test-tweet me by typing into your phone "@brooke_warner. I'm tweeting you from my phone!"

Pinterest

Pinterest is the fastest-growing social media site out there right now, and I predict that it will be on par with Facebook and Twitter by 2013 in terms of its value to publishers.

I finally decided to add Pinterest to my social media repertoire after months of procrastinating, in part because I didn't want to include anything else, and in part because I felt that I wasn't as on top of Facebook and Twitter as I needed to be. Once I got into a routine with Facebook and Twitter, I added Pinterest.

So far, I'm still playing with it, but I like it a lot. It's a site that allows you to create visual boards that highlight your interests. We've been talking a lot in this chapter about ways to turn readers on to your content, and Pinterest has all the elements to create very compelling imagery around your writing. If you were writing a novel, it could be fun to create a board for your protagonist, for instance, sharing with your followers the things she or he likes. You can also post video to your boards, so you can share theme songs or other training videos or interviews with your favorite authors.

If you're using Pinterest to grow your platform, you want to showcase things that are relevant to your topics and to your writing life, but I would make a case for sharing some personal content here. In creating a following, it's a good idea on Pinterest and any social media site to share some personal details about things you like, your family, and other small points of interest. This is for the purpose of connecting with your readers about things they care about, but it should also be only as personal as you are comfortable sharing. I have a board on Pinterest, for instance, called "Things My Toddler Loves." I like posting about James from time to time because I work with a lot of moms who are writers. For me, this is a way to connect with my readers and share some information about myself as a mom—something I feel really comfortable doing and something that lots of my followers respond to.

YouTube

You've probably watched videos on YouTube, but once you start building your platform using it, you will want and need to create your own YouTube channel. This is actually quite easy, and a lot of fun. This approach makes the most sense for authors writing prescriptive books, who can share their skills, methods, ideas, and inspirations. But it can also be useful for creative and mediagenic memoirists and novelists. You can act out little skits if you're a performer. You can read excerpts from your writing. You can post video of yourself speaking at an event or reading in front of an audience. You do want the content to be compelling, and fairly short. I try to keep all of my YouTube videos to under two minutes. The only exception to that rule is a tutorial I created on how to use Microsoft Word's Track Changes, which ended up being seven minutes.

If you cook, quilt, teach, dance, or do yoga or anything else that lends itself to video (and it's the topic of your book!), create video content. Video is exponentially more likely than written content to be shared and to go viral. People love video, and if they like something they watch, they'll probably come back and watch more.

I launched my YouTube channel when I decided to write this book, both to keep myself on top of my deadline and because I wanted to experiment with YouTube. When I first started posting videos, I was very self-conscious about being on camera. Now I feel comfortable, and I've learned how to keep my messages concise. I named my channel "Write with Brooke," and once my book is no longer at the top of my agenda, I intend to post writing and publishing tips to keep my presence there ongoing. Check out my YouTube channel at Youtube.com/warnercoaching.

LinkedIn

LinkedIn is all the rage with businesspeople. It's the premier networking site, especially business-to-business. LinkedIn can be a very valuable tool for prescriptive writers looking to connect with groups of people who would be a natural target audience for their book. For instance, LinkedIn hosts any number of publishing and writing groups; I'm a member of at least eleven of them. I have already started posting here and there little bits of information about who I am and what I'm doing, but once my book is available, I will be more active on these boards.

LinkedIn groups make sense for you if you're writing a niche book and can find an audience of people dedicated to talking about that topic there. You might be writing about word working, or temporary art, or raw food, or being the mom of twins. All of these topics lend themselves to special-interest kinds of groups, and you can generally find any special-interest group on LinkedIn. This is a site to take advantage of and become active on in the months leading up to your book's availability.

If you don't have an account, sign up for one today and link it to your Facebook account. Just like with Twitter, you can feed your Facebook posts to LinkedIn when you're just getting started.

Tumblr

Tumblr is a popular microblogging platform for people who really don't want to post a lot of content but have photos and images to share. I do think that Tumblr will be less and less relevant as Pinterest continues to explode onto the scene, but it's a popular blogging site, and it can be a good alternative to a WordPress site if—and only if—you think the idea of a WordPress site is too overwhelming. Most people have a Tumblr site in addition to their WordPress site.

Google+

Google+ is way less popular than Facebook, but because it's owned by Google, I see a future where it may edge Facebook out of the market. We'll see! I personally don't spend any time on Google+ because it's last on my social media priority list. Its primary interesting feature is that it organizes who you know by how you know them with a feature called "friend circles." This is nice because you can share information selectively with only certain groups of people. I enjoy getting Google+ round-ups, which are emails telling me what's popular on Google+, but since I rarely post there, I'm not otherwise too engaged. But, again, let's not write it off!

Understanding Social Media Strategy

I mentioned having read Michael Hyatt's book, *Platform: Get Noticed in a Noisy World,* as research for this chapter. I wanted to share with you his social media strategy to give you a bit of context for how to think about your online presence.

Hyatt identifies these three components of social media:

1. Home Base: This is digital property you own and control. This is your blog, your website, or maybe even a self-hosted community, like Kamy Wicoff's SheWrites. com.

2. Embassies: These are sites where you have a registered profile—social media sites like Facebook, Twitter, Pinterest, and even blogs you follow. Hyatt writes that you need a "passport" to visit these sites so that the site owner(s) will grant you access and allow you to participate there.

3. Outposts: These are all the places online where you just listen in. Google Alerts, for instance, is an outpost. Outposts are any sites that allow you to gather information about yourself or your company, or to monitor what's going on. Twitter's "#Discover" function is an outpost within an embassy because it allows you to find information based on key words and to monitor information that's relevant and self-serving (in a good way, of course).

Branding

The number one thing to know about branding is that you're conveying a message about who you are, and you drive home that message through consistency. Your color choices, the energy of any photos or images you select, your narrative voice, and the keywords you use are all part of your branding. By extension, your logo, your head shot, the banner of your website, your background images on your social media sites, and your business cards are all part of your branding. A potential reader should be able to look at any component of what you are putting out into the world to represent yourself: your message, your business, your book, and feel that they are seeing something that makes sense.

People who are all over the place with inconsistent branding don't realize that the subtle effect it has on their audience is a sense of disconnect. Your readership is going to start to feel that they have a mental and emotional picture of who you are the more they read your work, and you want to be the one in charge of what this image is by making use of all the different elements I've listed above.

Be Consistent

Consistency is about propagating the message you put out into the world about who you are. Consistency can be hard for some authors who want to be noticed for all that they are—similar to the memoirists mentioned above who struggle with the idea that they might be pigeonholed. But where branding is concerned, having a persona is part of the deal. You can start by coming up with keywords that describe who you are (or how you want to be perceived) as an author and what your message is about.

The issue of consistency came up from time to time with Seal authors who were writing about feminist topics. Feminism is an inherently edgy world. Women who take up the mantle of feminism tend to have to persevere against some pretty harsh voices from the Left and the Right who either are antifeminist or don't understand what feminism means. I had a number of authors who dealt with this brilliantly, who built up rather hardcore images around their work and their persona. But occasionally I worked with "softer" feminist writers who would want to be recognized for some other aspect of their personality, like one author who felt that her spirituality was part of her feminism.

It's not that these two things can't coexist. They certainly do. But what happened in the case of this particular author is that her readers didn't give two hoots about her spirituality because they'd gravitated to her for her feminism. When she posted more spiritual content on her site, people didn't get it. I won't go so far as to say they felt betrayed, but it was confusing. There was no context. And the posts themselves had an edge of self-indulgence to them because they clearly weren't for her target audience. Instead, they were for her. They were off brand, and while they might have made her feel more complete somehow, her audience didn't know what to make of them, and they were among the least popular posts she'd ever done.

Bring Your Email Address into the Twenty-first Century

If you still have a hotmail.com, earthlink.net, aol.com, or sbcglobal.net email address, this is an intervention. I empathize with your plight, I really do. I only updated my email address from b.warner@earthlink.net to brooke@warnercoaching.com at the end of 2011. I was worried about switching email accounts. I'd had that Earthlink account for so long, and I was nervous about all the many accounts I'd started that were associated with that email address.

The problem is what these addresses say about you. They say that you're stuck in the past—which in the technological age is really just a few years ago. But still, you're stuck. The only "generic" email address that's considered okay at this stage of the game is gmail.com, because Google is popular and has a good reputation, and people who use Google are seen as savvy.

So yes, it's time. Either get a gmail.com email address or get an email address that's associated with your domain name. If you buy your own name as your URL, the best convention is to use firstname@firstnamelastname.com. If you're worried that people will be able to guess your email address, you can change it up, but do not use something like me@firstnamelastname.com. When someone types this in, they are thinking about "me"—as in themselves. GoDaddy and any other hosting service allows you to create personalized email addresses associated with your URL for no additional charge, so if you already have a URL, there's no reason for you not to have an email address associated with that URL.

Make Your Signature Line Work for You!

Not having a signature line is a wasted opportunity to showcase what you're up to and to share, at least, your social media links. As of the writing of this book, my signature line reads:

> facebook.com/warnercoaching
> twitter.com/brooke_warner
> pinterest.com/warnercoaching
>
> Follow me while I write my book in six months (February–July) at Youtube.com/warnercoaching
>
> Sign up for Brooke's newsletter and get a free copy of "8 Strategies for Writing & Publishing Success" at www.warnercoaching.com
>
> "Anything or anyone that does not bring you alive is too small for you." —David Whyte

This is probably on the long end of what a signature line should include, but I wanted to showcase my Facebook, Twitter, and Pinterest pages. I also have wanted people to find my YouTube channel to watch me talk about my commitment to finish this book in six months. That will get removed as I wind down this journey. And I want to let people know that they can get my free report if they sign up for my newsletter. Finally, I feel it's important to include this quote from David Whyte, which has always been a source of inspiration for me, and which has been on my website since I first launched it in 2007.

You can decide what's important for you to highlight, but as you start to make yourself more visible, you want to put your signature line to work. It's an easy way to remind people what you're doing and where they can find you.

Get Bylines to Add to Your Credibility

It doesn't matter whether it's an op-ed or a feature piece—get your work published. The more bylines you have, the stronger your author profile. End of story. If you can say you've been published, you can include this information in your pitch letter and your proposal, and you'll have a leg up on the competition.

Start small. Publish for free in the beginning if you have to. Start researching where stories or articles that are relevant to your book might get picked up. This is hard work, particularly when the content you want to be writing is content for your book! However, publishing excerpts of your book as you go will not hurt your chances of getting published on a traditional press. I've worked on memoirs that had as many as five or six pieces previously published (usually in slightly different forms). Being published will help you get publishers' attention, and it's a surefire and easy way to strengthen your platform.

Endorsements Matter!

Endorsements, commonly referred to as "blurbs," have been a much-disputed staple in the publishing world. As anyone who's ever picked up a book knows, blurbs are part of a book's package. It's a tradition that many editors have a love/hate relationship with because obtaining blurbs is hard work. It requires pulling favors and oftentimes soliciting the same authors over and over.

For unpublished authors who are trying to shop their

book to agents and editors, however, getting advance blurbs by recognizable names can make a huge impression. Securing a foreword by someone well known can sometimes tip the scales in your favor where getting a publishing deal is concerned. You want these blurbs to be from authors of published books that have performed at least modestly well, or better. And celebrity endorsements are fine, of course! A blurb by a completely unknown author won't necessarily help you, but it won't hurt, either. You simply want to consider how to showcase those blurbs in your proposal. If you have a blurb by a big name, put it front and center on your website and on the title page of your proposal. Make sure to include the author's or celebrity's name and their accreditation: "author of [title of their book]" or "actress." List their show if they're not particularly in the public eye. If the endorser is not well known, put the blurb in your marketing section. Be careful not to include too many blurbs by unknown people. Three is usually a good number.

If you're writing a prescriptive book, industry people can provide good endorsements. Consider asking a person who's affiliated with a relevant organization, for instance. This is another good reason to make connections with organizations. Share information about your book with key people early on, so that you can circle back around and ask them for the favor of endorsing your book when the time comes. It's a gutsy thing to do to ask people for this favor, so if you don't feel comfortable asking people for favors, you'll have to step outside of your comfort zone. Blurbs are important to the book publishing world, and having early endorsements shows editors and agents that you're already a savvy author—since it takes sharing your work, asking for the favor, and having good connections.

Tip: Do not share endorsements from Twitter fans or endorsements in the form of responses to your blog or Facebook posts. I've seen this often enough, and I think authors largely think they're being clever. It doesn't impress authors and agents, though, even if it's a big name. There's a convention to getting endorsements that requires that the endorser receive a digital or hard copy of your book, read it (or at least browse it), and then provide you with the endorsement. Don't try to reinvent the wheel.

Contact Your Friends (or Friends of Friends) in High Places

Earlier on in this chapter I suggested you ask yourself the question: Are you connected to any organizations or "loudmouths" (people who like to spread the word about stuff) who could help you promote your book? You want to make a thorough list of people and organizations you're directly connected to, and then make a list of people and organizations you have a second-degree connection to. If you start this early on in your writing process, you can start cultivating relationships with people who might be natural promoters of your book. This isn't brownnosing or being manipulative. It's networking!

Go more deeply than just who you know, too. Who do you have access to? This isn't just about high-profile authors, celebrities, or heads of organizations. It's also about your potential readers. Think about your target audience. Where do they hang out and how can you reach them? Contacting people in high places might look like contacting people who run successful blogs and asking them if you can post on their site. You're trying to reach beyond your own sphere of influence and into other spheres. This is just as important for growing your platform as it is for the promotion of your future book. It used to be the case that everything we're talking about now was something you did once your book had been signed on with a publisher. Now you do all this legwork in order to prove yourself so that you can get signed on by a publisher.

Working your contacts can be hard for writers, particularly those who prefer to be at their computers writing, rather than engaging with the public. But publishers love authors who are out there engaging their readers— and working their connections. This doesn't mean you can't get published if you're not a social butterfly. But it's true that it's no longer possible to be a successful author if you refuse interviews, or live in relative obscurity, or are too shy to ask your friends who they know and whether they'd be willing to help you promote your book once it's out. Getting on people's radar is one thing. Securing their help is quite another—and this is the level you need to be at when you're truly thinking about your author platform and your role in the marketing campaign that's an inherent part of selling your book.

How One Self-Published Author Built Her Own Platform from Scratch and Sold Tons of Books

I interviewed author Rosie Sorenson in 2009 for advice for self-published authors about marketing and promoting because she'd done such an amazing job with her own book, *They Had Me at Meow: Tails of Love from the Homeless Cats of Buster Hollow,* a memoir about her thirteen years of caring for a colony of homeless cats. I am repurposing that interview here (with updates to bring it current) because it's timeless, and because it leads authors through one author's successful and well-executed process.

1. Set up a website and joined social networking sites. Rosie's site is TheyHadMeAtMeow.com. She's also on Facebook, Twitter, LinkedIn, and YouTube, and set up a page on the Poets and Writers website. Rosie has a readership of over twenty thousand for her humor column in the *Foolish Times.*

2. Created unique video content of some of her cats and posted them to YouTube. Rosie created a book trailer that included some of the cats featured in her books. In addition to being on YouTube, the videos are also on her website. She also set up an online store (Zazzle.com/theyhadmeatmeow) to sell mugs, T-shirts, greeting cards, and more featuring funny photos of the Buster Hollow Cats. She won the Muse Medallion Award from the Cat Writers' Association in 2010 for her humorous cards.

3. Sent the book out for early endorsement. Rosie sent the book to prominent people in the book's area of interest. Among them were the cat program manager of the

Humane Society of the United States, who ended up writing the foreword, and the founder and former director of Fix Our Ferals, in Berkeley, who wrote an introduction.

4. Set up her own book readings. Rosie organized a reading at her local independent bookstore as a benefit for Fix Our Ferals, the Humane Society of the United States, the Marin Humane Society, and Marin Cat Connection. She invited representatives from each of these organizations to appear with her on a panel. In addition to reading from her book, she also presented a funny slide show accompanied by Rob Laufer's song "In the Frame," for which she sought and received his permission. Eighty people attended, and she sold thirty-five books. She also organized readings at a Barnes & Noble in Oakland, California, as well as for two rescue organizations.

5. Secured sponsors. Rosie sold books in quantity to individuals who then donated them to rescue groups for community outreach, humane education, and fundraising. This isn't possible for every book, but if you have a book with a cause, setting up sponsorship can be a wonderful way to get more promotional copies out into the world.

6. Entered her book in contests. In 2009, Rosie won the Muse Medallion Award from the Cat Writers' Association. In 2010, she won the Best Pets Book award from the San Francisco Bay Area Independent Publishers Association.

7. Pitched herself to TV and radio. Rosie appeared on a San Francisco Bay Area show, *Bay Area People*, on KTVU-2. The broadcast is available on YouTube, which Rosie highlights on her website. Rosie did a radio interview with Bonnie Coleen's program, *Seeing Beyond*, which is broadcast throughout Northern California. She was also interviewed on *Conscious Dimensions* and has posted a link to the audio on her website. Radio opportunities are vast, and pitching yourself to a radio show that's in line with your audience can be a stepping-stone to other publicity opportunities.

8. Sent out post-publication copies for more endorsements and reviews. Rosie was able to garner more accolades for her book once it was out. She received glowing reviews from bestselling author and animal activist Jeffrey Moussaieff Masson; Ed Asner, actor; Catherine Coulter, author of fifty bestselling novels; and Lynette Evans, former editor at the *San Francisco Chronicle*. Sally Rosenthal, book editor, *Best Friends* magazine, said, "*Meow* . . . is one of the best cat books I've read in years."
Her book also received very favorable reviews from *Self-Publishing Review*, on Examiner.com, and on several prominent blogs about cats. Also, the *New York Daily News*, on September 9, 2009, included *Meow* in its list of nine great fall reads about animals.

9. Followed up on leads that resulted from these stories. The communications director of Alley Cat Rescue in Maryland contacted Rosie as a result of these stories, which led to her being featured in their newsletter (sixty thousand members strong!). Rosie is now a guest blogger for their website.

10. Keeps copies of her book on her at all times. Rosie has given away about 150 copies of her book for marketing purposes. She recently ran into Halle Berry at a restaurant in Berkeley and struck up a conversation with her about her book. Halle told Rosie she had four cats, and Rosie, on the ball, offered Halle an autographed copy of her book. She also met Portia de Rossi at a B&N book signing and gave her a copy of *Meow*. You never know who you'll meet, or where. So be prepared!

11. Makes future plans. Rosie is now working on an ebook version of *Meow,* adding new stories and photos, as well as links to videos she produced of the cats. She also plans to include some of the heartfelt emails she has received from her readers.

Rosie has been an incredibly active self-promoter who's found a way to get her very niche book out to hundreds of people. She's done a tremendous job at identifying her audience and focusing her attention on those people who care about cats as much as she does. This is part of the key to success. Don't dilute your efforts. Know your audience and go after them.

Multimedia Is a Must

Podcasts, radio interviews, YouTube and Vimeo uploads, vlogs, TV footage, and anything else you can think of that engages the reader with your image and your voice are essential to growing your author platform. Publicists and marketing people know that video is more likely to go viral than a blog post. The reason is simple, and it has to do with people's attention spans. YouTube has hundreds of millions of subscribers from all around the world, according to their own measures, and, they state, "forty-eight hours of video are uploaded every minute, resulting in nearly eight years of content uploaded every day." That's a lot of content, but there's a reason for it, too: People watch videos, and it's an easy way to connect to your audience.

The other benefit of doing podcasts and vlogs is that your readers get to know you on a totally different level when they can hear your voice and see your face. If you feel uncomfortable in front of the camera, do radio or audio. Try to get interviewed, even if it's by a small venue. You can use those clips on your website to draw people into your work and to grow your following. You talk about the same things I suggested you write about earlier in this chapter. Brainstorm ideas for one- to two-minute video clips, or five-minute audio segments. The point here is to experiment and find new ways to draw readers to you. This is what growing a platform is all about. Also, where shopping a proposal is concerned, showcasing that you understand the value of multimedia serves you in many ways. Your primary goal with everything you do en route to traditional publishing is to show how and why you're a desirable and collaborative partner in the publishing process. For a self-published author, it's just good business.

Speaking

Being able to show events that you have scheduled and/ or being able to show a list of venues where you've spoken or organizations you've spoken to is a huge component of your author platform. Aspiring authors who speak regularly can easily make a case that they'll do more speaking in the future. Since a book is a calling card, it's also very likely that having a book will increase the number of invitations you get to speak. This can be a bit difficult for new authors because they need the book to get the gigs, but even small gigs look good in a proposal. It's fine to say that you've spoken to a local school or nonprofit. I've spoken to countless writers' groups over the years. The most well-attended meeting I ever spoke at had about forty-five people; on average, I'd say the numbers have been closer to fifteen to twenty. But I've done them often and regularly, and I wouldn't hesitate to list those speaking engagements in a book proposal.

If you're doing a lot of speaking, make sure to have a tab on your website. Create a media packet, and include this information in your book proposal. Make it easy for people to find out what you have to offer. Just like everything we've been discussing in this chapter, public speaking is not necessarily for everyone. You might feel that you don't have anything to offer. Again, the novelists and memoirists among you may be struggling to wrap your minds around how to go about getting public speaking events. But you can get them, and you start in the same way you start thinking about how you're going to become the go-to person on your topic. You have to start shifting your mentality when you decide you want to publish. You are a specialist on something—whether you're writing about having a personality disorder, about growing up a child of alcoholic parents, a paranormal fairy tale, or a character-driven story about a young couple who go through fertility treatments and end up having septuplets.

I can't think of a single book out there whose author is not a candidate for speaking. And if you're stumped, I invite you to pose the question of what you could be posting about or speaking about to my Facebook page so that I can help you brainstorm and get you thinking like a published author.

CONCLUSION: GENEROSITY IS THE NEW CURRENCY

Kamy Wicoff, founder of SheWrites.com and my cofounder in She Writes Press, says this: "Generosity is the new currency." This statement could easily become your new mantra where platform is concerned. Everything you do around your blog, social media, and speaking is about sharing what you know. The more you can share and give to people, the more they're interested in what you have to say. According to marketing experts, you have to "touch" people eight times before they're even interested in listening. Beyond that, you have to have many more opportunities for engagement and trust building before someone wants to buy something from you.

This is the value of being out there, of making your voice heard. And granted, it's not easy. It is a noisy world out there. There are other people doing what you're doing, and yet you can't let this make you feel defeated. The lasting voices are the ones who never give up, who know they have good content and a lot to say. Your author platform is not just about one book. It's your journey toward becoming a go-to person, a thought leader, an expert in your genre. The most popular novelists and memoirists today are teaching about craft, about what they've learned through publishing many books, about the writing process.

If you want to write, you have to consider the many talents you have beyond writing. Why do you write? What deeper truth do you want to share? What's universal about your story, and what impact will it make on others? These are the probing questions writers should consider when they're thinking about their author platform. Who do you want to join you in conversation—about your topic, your area of interest or expertise—and how do you want that conversation to go? This is about framing a conversation and the issues you care about. Everything you put out into the world, therefore, should be deliberate; it should matter to you; it should serve a purpose. If it's a throwaway thing to you, it's a throwaway thing to your audience, too.

People know generosity when they see it. They can feel it, and even if it's only in the form of great content or a valuable message, they feel seen, understood, and held. This is your charge to your readership, and this is what building a good platform, when it's done right, should achieve. From here, your following will be created and expanded upon, and should be cultivated as the most valuable asset you have.

Chapter 5.
Your Publishing Plan:
A Strategic Road Map to Becoming a Published Author

Whenever I start working with a new client, I always want to know what their publishing ambitions are. Some writers are crystal clear about their desire to publish; others seem to want to tiptoe around it, as if owning their ambitions or desires will jinx them. Plenty of writers—often women—have been conditioned to curb their dreams, the result of direct and indirect messaging that women should not be too much or too intense, should not dream too big, should not want so much or aim so high.

In my work with writers, I'm all about aiming high. The message "don't get your hopes up" is ultimately about fear of the letdown being too big. It's easier to pick yourself up off the floor if you expect the worst, if you don't allow yourself to feel into the probability of what's possible. And yet if we don't dream big, how can we ever realize what we truly want, what we believe is possible? When it comes to our publishing dreams, who hasn't experienced that little spark of possibility? What if I can sell my book to an agent or editor who loves it? What if my book is so well received that it becomes a bestseller? What if my writing can allow me to leave my day job? What if I become a famous author? And why would you even want to deny yourself access to the possibility that any of these things might be possible?

In my opinion, these dreams are good dreams to have because they're motivating—but they ultimately best serve you when they're paired with buckling down and doing the work required to manifest them. It's the rare author who comes out with a first book that allows them to become a full-time writer. And yet there are those flukes—books like the 2011 blockbuster *Fifty Shades of Grey*—that make the author a runaway success even though they're not a particularly good writer, and even though they weren't known previously. Because of that mystery factor, publishing can feel a little like a gamble: You might be the lucky winner of a six-figure publishing deal, a bestselling book, and a full-time writing career! But for the vast majority of us, this is not how it works.

Most of us, instead, need a publishing plan, which is what we're going to be covering in this chapter. Because the publishing industry is both complicated to navigate and changing so quickly, the best way to approach your publishing plan is with flexibility, optimism, and good humor. In this chapter, I'm going to offer you a road map to understanding your options. Which path you choose is up to you, of course, but giving up on your book is not an option. My hope is that by the end of this chapter you'll feel motivated enough to try to get traditionally published if you determine that you have what it takes to do so, or inspired enough to self-publish when you discover a few things about self-publishing that you might not have known.

PITCHING AND SHOPPING

Before we talk about your publishing plan, I want to spend a moment on pitching and shopping and what all these two activities entail. Most writers, once they decide they're interested in getting published, go online and start to do some research. One of the first things you'll likely find is a writers' conference in your area, or something called a Pitchfest. Although I believe the earliest writers' conferences started for the purposes of gathering like-minded people together to talk about and teach writing, today's conferences are so focused on the pitch that newbie aspiring authors are sometimes led to believe that all they need to do is perfect their pitch and they'll get a publishing deal. Your pitch is like a short advertisement for your book. It's actually not that different—if at all different—from a query letter. The only difference is that the pitch is given verbally and the query letter is written.

Another thing you'll likely come across in your research are writers blogging about shopping their book, or editors or coaches like me blogging about things you need to know when shopping your book. When you hear someone talking about shopping a project, they're referring to sending the work out to agents or editors. This is the only way to shop your work. If you're self-publishing, you don't shop. You may look for a good self-publishing partner, but shopping refers to landing an agent or an editor. You are, in effect, selling your book (or your proposal, with the promise to complete your book) in exchange for a publishing deal (that hopefully includes an advance).

Pitch It!

The pitch is not so different from a movie trailer. It exists to entice the person listening to want to know more. Just like a query letter, the pitch opens with a hook, gives a short narrative summary of the book, and ends with something that leaves us wanting more. Creating a good pitch takes a lot of effort, and I'm not suggesting that what I perceive to be an overemphasis on the pitch makes it an unworthy exercise. I'm simply asserting that even a great pitch does not guarantee a book contract. What it can do is open up doors and get you reads from agents and editors.

The real value of the pitch is in the way it positions your book. Positioning has to do with where your book belongs in the marketplace, and the real work of it begins with the pitch. A good pitch tells your agent exactly how to present you to an editor, and tells the editor how to present you to their sales force, and tells the sales force how to present you to your readers. A well-written pitch will serve as copy for Amazon, the in-house catalog, publicity releases, and your back cover. The earlier you can nail down solid content and a strong message, the better the selling tools you will have for your book. And remember, it has to do with perception. You want to make your book sound like a book people will want to read, just as a movie trailer makes you want to go see the movie.

The reason pitching has become such an industry in and of itself is because of Pitchfests and writers' conferences, where aspiring authors pay money to get face time with agents and authors. I have attended countless conferences and heard hundreds, if not thousands, of pitches over the years, and the value of getting face time with an agent or editor cannot be overstated. The fact that this cottage industry of conferences exists and that agents and editors attend them is actually a very cool thing. Agents and editors go to conferences because they hope to find a diamond in the rough, but the truth is that the majority of writers are not ready to shop their manuscripts when they begin to seek out writers' conferences.

By the time you're really ready to shop your work, you will be savvier than the average conferencegoer. You will have won conference awards, and maybe you'll be invited to sit on a panel instead of being in the audience. For those of you who are just beginning to think about publishing, go to a conference. Get educated. Take notes. Ask good questions. Get feedback about your pitch—what's working and not working. But don't think that just because an agent or editor says they'll look at your work, it's an automatic slam dunk.

I like to remind nervous authors that agents and editors are at those conferences to find projects, so treat them as you would someone who wants to partner with you. And take their feedback in stride. Sometimes an agent or editor is not going to get what you're doing, and that's fine. Authors who argue with an agent or editor about why their book is a good fit for them are an automatic red flag. You want to be confident, but not aggressive. If you get an invitation to submit, be gracious and prepare for that submission as you would for something you desperately want.

How Badly Do You Want It?

Think of something in your life you've really really really wanted. Maybe it was a scholarship, or a job, or admission to a particular college or program. Getting your book published on a traditional press ranks up there with the most important things you've gone after in your life, because the barriers to entry are very high, and so is the competition. You can't buy your way in. You have to earn it, and you have to offer yourself as a collaborative and savvy business partner.

I was often shocked, in reviewing proposals I received as an acquisitions editor, by many authors' hastiness. Because books can be sold on proposal, some writers want to get the commitment before they do the hard work. Writing a book can be fun, rewarding, and fulfilling, but it's the opposite of instant gratification. The work of getting a manuscript or a book proposal ready to shop is no small thing, and oftentimes, even after you find an agent or land at a publishing house, there's a whole other round of editorial considerations to account for.

Do your homework when deciding whom to submit to and where to submit. Take your proposal very, very seriously, and make sure you're following proposal guidelines and that you submit according to the rules of the agency or publishing house you're submitting to. Don't be anxious and jump the gun. The publishing world will still be there a year from now. If you need to work out the kinks in your novel, do it before you shop. If you know you need to build your platform, take three or six months or more to do it. If you go out too early, chances are, you won't be able to circle back around to those agents and editors who rejected you the first time out of the gate. Gather up information and learn about how things work. Take your time and become an expert. If getting published on a traditional press is what you really really want, it will be there waiting for you when you're really really ready.

Shop It!

You're ready to shop your book once you either (a) have a complete manuscript or (b) have a complete proposal and sample chapters. It's required that novelists be finished with their project before shopping, but that's not the case for nonfiction writers. Nonfiction writers are always invited to submit their work on proposal, meaning that you must create a comprehensive nonfiction book proposal that includes the following components:

- Title Page
- Overview (aka Summary)
- Proposal Table of Contents
- Chapter-by-Chapter Summaries
- Author Biography
- Marketing/Publicity
- Target Audience
- Competitive Titles
- Sample Chapters

Although I am not going to get into what each of these components entails, I invite you to Google "Create a Winning Nonfiction Book Proposal with Brooke Warner," which is a free step-by-step action plan for nonfiction writers (memoir and prescriptive) to create a nonfiction book proposal, complete with samples that went on to get published—along with tips and best practices.

The minimum number of sample chapters you can shop is generally two, but if you're a person who's looking for that instant gratification, I would recommend writing more rather than less. The fact is that if an agent or an editor is interested in your work, they're going to ask to see more material. You don't want to be caught off-guard in that moment. It never looks good to have to write back, "Oh, great, I'm so glad you're interested. Now let me write Chapter 3." At the outset of this chapter, I wrote that not publishing should not be an option, so for those of you thinking that you'll wait and see if someone is interested in your project and let that determine whether or not you'll finish, you might want to spend some time asking yourself how invested you really are in what you're doing. You have to find that internal drive, whether you end up with a publisher or not, so writing more chapters even though you're not required to is a great way to measure your own passion for what you're doing.

Shopping to an agent or an editor is a straightforward process that involves the following steps:

1. Email the agent or the editor by querying them. Find out their name. Do not send your query letter to a general inbox if you can avoid it. It's easy to research the name of an agent or editor online. (Please see Resources for more on this.) You cut and paste your query letter (the written version of your pitch) into the body of the email. The last line of the query asks for permission to send the proposal (if you're writing nonfiction) or the first fifty pages of your novel (if you're writing fiction). It looks like this: "My proposal is complete. May I send it to you?" Or: "My novel is complete. May I send you the first fifty pages?"

2. At this point, one of three things happens: (1) you get a response from the agent or editor saying yes, they'd like to

see more; (2) you get a response from the agent or editor saying they're not interested; or (3) you don't hear back. If you got a positive response, move on to point 3 in this list. If you got a no or if you didn't hear back, you still have options. If you got a no with no explanation, it's okay to write back and ask for more feedback. The worst thing that can happen is that the agent or editor won't write back. The best thing is that they will give you more information. I've often encouraged authors to ask agents and editors if they know anyone in the industry whom they might recommend. You never know. Book publishing people are very friendly folks, and if they like you and your project but can't take it on, they may still be interested in helping you. If you get no response, all you can do is follow up a few more times. Follow up once after four weeks, and again after six. After that, there's not much else you can do.

3. If the agent or editor says yes, congratulations. This is worth celebrating. It means you have a good query letter and the agent or editor is interested enough that they're going to read your proposal. You write back a very simple response thanking them and attaching your proposal or the first fifty pages of your work. Novelists, I recommend submitting a chapter-by-chapter summary of your novel. This is not required, but it goes a long way, and I've never met an agent or an editor who doesn't appreciate the extra step in helping them see the arc of the whole work.

4. At this point you will wait, and the same three things can happen: (1) you get a response from the agent or editor

saying yes, they'd like to represent you or publish your book; (2) you get a response from the agent or editor saying they're not interested; or (3) you don't hear back. If you get a positive response, move on to point 5 in this list. If you get a no or don't hear back, you also have options. If you get a no, I would encourage you to write and ask for more feedback if you're not satisfied with their response, though often agents and editors provide thorough reasons for why they can't take a book on. Whatever you do, don't argue with them or try to convince them of all the reasons they should take you on. It will not change their mind. If you get no response, you can email a few times to see what's up, but I would argue that you probably don't want to work with an agent or editor who cannot get back to you after they've already agreed to look at your project. In my opinion, this is bad form. It typically takes four to six weeks for an agent or editor to get back to you, after which point you should follow up with a short check-in email asking the agent or editor if they've had time to review your work.

5. If you've gotten an offer from an agent or editor, you get to celebrate. But it's not quite over. You do need to tie up the loose ends. Do not say yes right away. The offer will not disappear just because you need a little time to think about it. You want to use this time to circle back around to other agents or editors and let them know that you have an offer. If you have more than one agent or house interested, you want to get on the phone with those people and just talk. You want to like the person you're entering into a relationship with. Ask them about their communication style, and if they

have an editorial vision for your book. Even though this is an enviable position to be in, you still want to do your homework and see everything through. Once you've accepted representation or a book contract, you need to inform all the other agents or editors you submitted to that you have found representation or found a home for your work.

The main thing to know about this five-step process is that it's not fast, although it can be. You want to get organized by keeping some sort of spreadsheet about whom you've submitted to, when, what their response was, and all the relevant dates. You also want to start small. I recommend submitting to no more than ten agents or editors in your first pass. You never know what the response will be, and you want to be able to have the bandwidth and attention to attend to the possibility that all ten agents will say yes. Once you've gotten some rejections, then you can start to gauge what works for you and how many lines of correspondence you feel you want to have open at any given time.

Very important note: Never submit to agents and editors at the same time. You must choose one or the other, and generally you will start with agents, unless you know you want to try to go directly to a publisher. We'll get into what your options are below, but you are going to either try to get agented or try to shop to an editor directly. If you shop to editors before you get an agent, you are doing the job for the agent. I've worked with several clients who shopped their book around to editors and got rejections. They then decided they would try to get an agent. They were elated when they got the interest of an agent, but once they told the agent that they had submitted to several presses and been rejected, the agent told them they couldn't represent the author. I've seen this happen multiple times in my coaching practice, and the authors are crestfallen, but what they've really done is cripple their agent's chances of selling their book, because once a house says no, it's very unlikely that you can circle back around to them and get a yes down the road on the same project. It's possible. I've seen it happen. But it's very rare.

YOUR PUBLISHING PLAN

I always tell writers I work with that anyone who tries hard enough and has enough tenacity can get published on a traditional publisher. But today more than ever, traditional publishing is not the best or only option for everyone. Your unique publishing plan has to do with your motivations for publishing in the first place, what you hope to achieve from having a published book, and how realistic you are.

When it comes to getting published, there are only three options: (1) get an agent and publish on a traditional press; (2) sell your work directly to an editor without an agent; and (3) self-publish. The only caveat worth mentioning here is that many writers sign with agents who cannot sell their work. Since a good plan always involves having a solid backup plan (or two), the fact that agented manuscripts don't sell has to factor into your equation.

So what should your plan look like? In order to get you oriented to what's in store for you, I'm going to lead you through a visualization. Imagine that you've come to the end of your book-writing journey (or, for some of you, to the end of your proposal). You find yourself in a crowded city, standing on a wide street that suddenly branches into three smaller streets, all lined with storefronts. Each of these streets is well-marked. To your left is Agents Way, the middle street is Publishers Row, and to your right is Self-Publishing Boulevard.

Your publishing plan from here has to do with how you want to explore these streets. If you're in pursuit of a traditional publishing deal, you start down Agents Way. This street has all kinds of storefronts—some very small, with just one person manning the front desk, and others quite large buildings with lots of people bustling around. You will knock on a lot of doors and make your way as far down this street as you want, until you are tired of it, or until you've exhausted all of your options. Once you get picked up by an agency, that's it. They invite you in and you come in off the street. At this point, you're in your agent's house and the two of you will partner to try to sell your work to a publishing house.

If no one invites you inside, you'll walk back to the spot where the street forked into three smaller streets and you'll make your way down Publishers Row. Here you'll see that some storefronts have their lights off and their doors closed. You are not allowed to approach every single building on this street. You are allowed to approach only those that accept unsolicited submissions. Random House, Simon & Schuster, HarperCollins, Harcourt, and a number of others will have a barricade around them. Only agents are allowed in. However, there are plenty of smaller houses that will be open to hearing from you.

You need a map for Publishers Row because you need to know what the various houses actually publish. Don't waste your time or the time of the people inside these publishing houses by presenting them with a project that's not right for them. This is a street you can spend a lot of time on, so take it slow and see what happens. And just like on Agents Way, once you're tired or you've exhausted your possibilities, you will make your way back to the crossroads.

For those of you who've already explored Agents Way and Publishers Row, standing at the fork and looking down Self-Publishing Boulevard might feel discouraging. But it shouldn't. Here, no one will turn you down. But it doesn't mean you shouldn't do your research. Every single door you walk through down this street will cost you money. You want to make sure you know where you want to hang out. You will be spending a lot of time behind one of these doors. You're paying them, too, so you want to make sure that you like how they present themselves, how they interact with you, and what they're offering. Every other doorway on this street is open to you, so don't feel like you have to be too hasty. Once you decide who you want to spend time with, you pass through the doorway, where you will stay until you have a published book.

Understanding your options, let's circle back around to the points above having to do with your motivations, what you hope to achieve, and how realistic you are. These points can help us engage in a process of elimination to help you decide whether you have the tolerance to explore all three streets. For some of you, Agents Way isn't going to be as appealing as Publishers Row. Others of you will bypass both of those streets and go straight to Self-Publishing Boulevard. Still others of you will be invited in by an agent on Agents Way, spend a long time there, and discover that nothing is happening, at which point you may have to leave of your own accord.

Let's figure out what your journey should look like now by starting with this question: What are your motivations for publishing in the first place? There are plenty of you who will answer that all that matters, above and beyond all else, is that your work be published. If you already feel this way, you're going to follow the plan I laid out above and you won't need to worry about modifying it. If you're a person who knows they will not and cannot self-publish, then you will only check out Agents Way and Publishers Row. If you succeed in getting an agent or an editor, then you're still in the game. If you don't and you don't want to explore Self-Publishing Boulevard, then you'll be pulling yourself out of the game. This is totally up to you, and, as I said, you can spend *a lot* of time on Publishers Row. In fact, you can spend a lot of time on Agents Way and Publishers Row—years, even. There are hundreds of agents and hundreds of publishers, and this is where tenacity comes into play. If you're committed and you do the work, eventually someone on one of those streets will open their door to you.

Next, what do you hope to achieve from having a published book? The vast majority of aspiring authors want to publish because it's a dream they've had for a long time.

They want to share their story. They generally believe that what they're writing will help people. Indeed, most often the desire to write a book is quite altruistic. However, there are those writers who want or need external validation, who hope that a book will give them some measure of fame and income. In my opinion, any of these streets can offer you what you're looking for, but you have to understand what you want and what your expectations are.

Agents Way is the equivalent of a glitzy street, kind of like Rodeo Drive. It's impressive and can be glamorous. You can feel like you're one of the chosen ones when someone invites you in and takes on your project. Publishers Row is a little more like Route 29 in Napa, California. It's more like being invited into someone's home, and some of them have a better reputation than others. Self-Publishing Boulevard is a little bit like the Strip in Vegas. There are shady spots and there are really good spots. There are places you might be embarrassed to be associated with, and there are really classy joints. But oftentimes you won't know until you walk inside and look around. If you've never been there before, you might also want to get a referral from a trusted friend.

Obviously, anyone can go walk around on Rodeo Drive, but some of you already know that you don't have the resources to shop there. For the nonfiction writers among you, resources here equal platform. As we discussed in Chapter 4, if you really want to make it all the way to a big offer from a big house, your platform needs to be amazing. On the other hand, some of the novelists among you might get swooped up in the flurry of a big agency and a big deal and not even know what's happened or how. Know that the rise to the top in publishing can be fun and rewarding, and can feel like a dream come true, but it sometimes comes with consequences. There are plenty of stories of authors who get six-figure deals on their first book, and then, when those books don't earn out (meaning the publisher doesn't earn their money back), the publishing house doesn't want to buy those authors' second book. I mention this only so that you keep up your guard and watch out for your career. Enjoy your success if you get a big offer from a big house, but don't take it for granted.

For others of you, Route 29 in Napa is going to feel more like the kind of place you imagine yourself being. You can already imagine cozying up with a publisher who really gets you, who wants to represent you for the long-term, who's going to give you a little bit more hand-holding. These kinds of experiences are rewarding for authors in large part because their expectations were more realistic from the get-go. Authors pursuing smaller houses don't go into the relationship thinking they want or need a six-figure deal. The books they're writing are generally more niche, so they land with a house where their editor is passionate about their project. Because these authors have done the work of placing themselves without an agent, they don't have the support of an agent, but they also don't have to give the 15 percent commission. Many small houses offer no advance, but some of them will offer in the range of $2,000, $5,000, or $10,000. Sometimes even more. Most authors I speak to, once they discover the differences between getting agented and pursuing a big house, versus shopping directly to a publisher, see the latter as a better fit for them. Small-press publishing does have legitimate upsides, though it necessarily comes with downsides, too, which we'll explore later on in this chapter.

Finally, there will be those of you who are excited by the notion of the Strip of publishing. Here the possibilities are endless. Here you can be a maverick. You can create your own rules and partner with whomever you want. If you do it right, the payoff can be tremendous. If you do it wrong, you can lose face and money. On Self-Publishing Boulevard, you have complete creative control. If you have a vision for your book, you can follow that through till the end. You can partner with a company that's more like a vanity press, that will let you do whatever you want, however you want, or you can publish with a hybrid company that requires that your project fit certain guidelines. Again, we'll expand upon the difference between vanity and hybrid presses below—as well as everything in between.

And there you have it. You know the streets and you can see how they unfold in front of you. You can pursue all of these streets or just one of them. I personally chose to go directly to Self-Publishing Boulevard because my motivations for publishing had to do with establishing myself in my field. I wanted and hoped to sell a lot of copies of this book, but my primary desire was to reach people who might be interested in working with me. I was not trying to reach the masses. Finally, when it comes to how realistic I was (and am)—I'm very realistic. Coming from a publishing background, I know what kind of platform it takes to get picked up by a big press. I didn't even bother exploring Agents Way at this juncture with this book. I think I could have found a publisher on Publishers Row, but I didn't have the time, and I wanted complete creative control. I already knew the title and subtitle I wanted. I already had a designer I wanted to work with. So for me, time and control factored into the equation. Thus, Self-Publishing Boulevard was a pretty clear choice for me, as it will be for many of you. And this can be a huge relief.

Words of Advice

1. Don't shop multiple agents in a single agency. This may seem obvious, but people do it all the time.

2. Don't feel like you have to shop to the president or head agent of the agency you're interested in shopping to. Although it may seem counterintuitive, it's often better to shop to a junior agent. They're generally more eager and hungry to grow their lists and shop projects, while the owners of the agencies have established client lists, often aren't taking on new clients, and simply don't have the same drive.

3. Shop agents in your region. If you live on the West Coast, find agencies out of California, Oregon, or Washington. If you're in the South, look at Texas or Florida. I'm not suggesting you bar New York options, but oftentimes people's work has a certain sensibility that's unique to their region of the country, and agents working out of that region of the country can have a better sense of how to shop and place the work. In my experience, New York agents often—though certainly not always—have their sights set on New York houses that are in the New York publishing bubble.

Agents Way: How to Get an Agent

As I mentioned above, getting an agent is the only way you can approach big houses. If you have a dream of publishing on what are known in the industry as the Big Six publishers—Random House, Simon & Schuster, Penguin, Hachette, HarperCollins, or Macmillan—you must be agented. And it's necessary to be agented in order to approach plenty of other houses, too. Publishers who take unsolicited (meaning unagented) manuscripts will say so on their site, or they'll specify that they do not. It's pretty easy to explore and discover how limited you might feel by not having an agent.

I've already outlined the process of pitching and shopping, so what I want to focus on here is how to find an agent, and questions to ask them once they express interest, as well as questions to ask yourself.

As I mentioned above, Agents Way is a jam-packed street with all different types of setups. You have huge agencies with multiple senior and junior agents; you have some that have three or four agents; and you have others that are just a single agent with their own list of clients. None of these setups is better or worse. You're going to need to cast your net wide, too, so it's a good idea to try a variety of different agencies and agents and see what turns up.

Now that you have some parameters, you need to know where to start looking. There are a number of good resources, though I believe the best, in this order, are:

1. Publishers Marketplace. Publishers Marketplace (PublishersMarketplace.com) is the best-known site for

tracking deals, and it's used by industry insiders to find agents and editors. With a $20/month membership, you have access to a database that gives you agents' names, email addresses, and information about what they're looking for, as well as their lists. Because the agents design their own landing pages on this site, you can get a clear idea of their sensibility.

2. *The Guide to Literary Agents.* This is a book that comes out annually, and a blog (WritersDigest.com/editor-blogs/guide-to-literary-agents) run by Chuck Sambuchino, the editor of the print edition. Depending on how you prefer to research, it can be worth it to get the hard-copy edition. You can also get last year's edition for a significant discount on Amazon, and generally not that much information changes from one year to the next. *The Guide to Literary Agents* is a lot like *The Big Book of Colleges,* which lists every college and its application process. It can be a lot to wade through, but it doesn't show you, like Publishers Marketplace does, who's making deals and selling projects.

3. 1000LiteraryAgents.com. This site has a free basic membership and seems to be a good backup to the other two resources. The site is a bit simplistic, which is actually nice, but there's no rhyme or reason to the sorting, which leads me to believe that agents who get good placement are probably paying for it.

Use these resources to compile a list of ten agents, as I mentioned above. You can certainly research more, but start by just choosing your top ten and seeing what hap-pens. Once you're ready, send your pitch and wait and see what happens. You'll get the yes, no, or radio silence, and you alone will decide how long you hang in with this process. How long you stay on Agents Way is certainly an unknown at the outset of the shopping process. You could be there a matter of weeks, or you could be there well past the time when you know you need to seek out another option.

If an agent reviews your proposal or your manuscript and makes an offer of representation, it's cause for cele-bration. No question. But *do not* say yes right away. You don't want to be locked into a relationship with that agent, no matter how excited you are, until you make sure that all the other channels that you opened up in your shopping process are closed. You will systematically go back to each and every agent you pitched and let them know that you have an offer of representation. If you are lucky and you have more than one agent interested in working with you, you need to act like a new graduate who's pursuing a job and has multiple companies courting them. This is in fact a courting process, and while you don't need to act like a diva about it, you are in the driver's seat, and you want to interview your prospective agent.

Signing with an agent is as big a deal as, or bigger than, signing with a publishing house, because this person (if all goes well) could be representing you for your entire career and for all future projects. You never want to sign with someone just because they say they like your work and they can sell your book. You need to get on the phone and make sure you (a) like them; (b) have a gut feeling that they really like and get your book; and (c) know what their editorial vision for your book is and how they plan to shop your book.

When you schedule that first phone call with your agent, ask them the following questions:

1. What's your agency fee?

The standard is 15 percent of the author's take, including advances and royalties; it might be as high as 20 percent if the agent is selling subrights (foreign, film, etc.), but never higher than that. Find out if subrights are handled by the agency, or whether they work with a third party. If you want to keep certain rights, such as merchandise or film/ TV (many authors do), bring that up early on.

2. What's your preferred method of communication?

This one is critical, because if you're a phone person and your agent is an email person, you might get very frustrated when you find out later that you will never have a verbal conversation. If you're a first-time author and you know you're going to have a lot of questions, ask the agent how he or she feels about that. You want to have a sense of the agent's boundaries early on and make sure that you won't be disappointed later if you're not getting the kind of attention you were hoping to get.

3. What do you envision for my book?

Always assume that some work will be needed on your

proposal/manuscript. Ask your would-be agent what they think your project's needs are and where they think improvements might be made. This is not a time to fish for compliments, but you should be listening for whether or not you feel like their vision for your project is the same as yours. Does their feedback resonate with you? If not, you really need to ask yourself if you will move forward with them anyway. I know so many authors whose proposals were changed in order to make their books more salable, but so much so that the author stopped feeling connected to their own book. Once that book gets published, you can feel real resentment. You might even feel that it's a book you wish you'd waited on. So a meeting of the minds is very important here.

4. What's your strategy for shopping my book?

Find out how the agent shops, or intends to shop. Will they only approach big houses, or will they consider small houses if you have a lead or an idea you want them to try? What kind of timeline do they have in mind in terms of when it might be ready to shop to publishers? You may be surprised to find out that they think your book requires a lot of work. They might not intend to shop the book for another year. You want all these things on the table before you sign a contract.

5. Do you anticipate any costs on my part in order to get the manuscript to a shoppable place?

Find out whether your would-be agent expects you to hire

a freelance editor at your own cost. As I mentioned above, an agent might want to take you on, but they have a vision for the book that requires you to partner with an editor—and the agency is not going to pay for this, of course. Find out if there are any other out-of-pocket expenses they are thinking about before you sign—and make sure you can live with whatever those things might be before you move forward.

After your interview or interviews, give yourself some time to sit with your decision. Yes, it's wonderful to have an offer, but remember, they're not going to pull the offer just because you want a day or two to think things over. Here are five questions you want to ask yourself before you sign with any agent:

1. Is this agent someone you can imagine working with through the good and the bad?

Remember, agents are mediators and advocates whose job requires not only fighting on your behalf, but also pushing back on you at times. Is this someone you can work with when the going gets tough?

2. How quickly does the agent respond to you?

This is an important one for people who are quick responders and expect that everyone else should be, too. If the agent confesses that it takes a while to respond to his or her emails, are you going to be okay with that?

3. What kinds of clients/projects do they represent?

Do your homework. Go to the agency website and find out what they represent and whether you like the books. Really, you should have done this before you even pitched them. Ask if they'll let you talk to one or two of their current clients to find out about those authors' experiences. This is not out of line or even remotely inappropriate. The worst thing they can say is no.

4. Can you envision this agent representing you for your entire career?

Make sure you're signing on for something that makes sense for where you are in your career. If you want to take it book by book, that's okay, and it's okay to ask for that. It's also okay to voice your expectations that you want to work with someone who wants to be with you for the long haul.

5. Do you understand the terms of the contract?

Make sure the payment provisions in the contract they're offering make sense to you, and don't hesitate to ask questions about things you don't understand. You don't want to find out post-signing that you're not okay with some of the language. Take your time and go through the contract slowly and deliberately.

Publishers Row: How to Partner with a Publisher

For many of you, Publishers Row will be a place you decide you're finally ready to explore because you haven't succeeded in finding an agent. Or maybe you did, but you didn't get a particularly good vibe from them, or you were agented and the agent was unable to sell your work. Some authors may bypass Agents Way altogether and start on Publishers Row. Maybe you have a connection—an "in"—to a particular publisher or an editor. This could be through a friend, or it could be because you met an editor at a writers' conference. Or maybe you just feel deep in your bones that your book is a perfect fit for a particular publisher's list. Regardless of your reasons, you're ready to approach a publishing house directly.

I started my publishing career at North Atlantic Books, a true small press. It is owned by a husband-and-wife team. It has an eclectic list, which for years was fairly representative of the publisher's personal interests and tastes. When I worked there, the press published about eighty books a year—a lot of titles for a small press. We generally offered little to no advance. The publisher preferred to work with unagented authors, and it was the rare book that came through that was attached to an agent. The authors who landed with North Atlantic Books fit a certain profile, for the most part. They were specialists, highly educated, and often well known within their particular niche (martial arts, paranormal sciences, somatic psychology, raw foods). They felt understood by the press and its employees, and the experience for them, while certainly not always perfect and blissful, was generally good. They were partnering with a publisher who got what they were about because, as a press, North Atlantic acquires books that align with a certain intellectual value system.

Next I worked at Seal Press, which used to be an independently owned small press but is now part of the Perseus Books Group, which, while not a Big Six publisher, is definitely a big press—considered midsize in the publishing world. It owns multiple imprints, and Seal Press is the smallest. Seal has maintained its small-press sensibility through acquisitions by bigger presses (first by Avalon Publishing Group and then by Perseus), which is something I've always loved about it, and a highlight about publishing with the press that I made sure to point out to authors I was trying to court. Seal's authors are also of a certain profile, but it has much more to do with being progressive, irreverent, informing of women's lives, and supportive of women. In Seal's case, the authors and/or the authors' books truly need to fit the press's mission statement. By and large, small presses tend to be more mission-driven than large presses, which we'll talk about a bit more later on in this section.

Authors can submit directly to Seal Press, and many did, but the number of books acquired through the submissions pile was abysmally low. During my time there, Seal published about forty books a year, and one of those books, if that, would have been an unsolicited manuscript. During my time at North Atlantic Books, however, the reverse was true. Small presses vary quite a bit in this regard. You're not more or less likely to get a publishing deal with a small press because you do or don't have an agent. It's more about understanding whether you are a fit for a particular press's list and then making your case. Sometimes agented authors will even pursue small-press deals without their agent, since they know it's more of a passion project than a moneymaking endeavor.

For instance, during my time at Seal, the authors of *The Guy's Guide to Feminism,* Michael Kimmel and Michael Kaufman, approached me with the idea for this book. They emailed me directly and pitched me on the concept of doing a book about feminism for men, written by men. Seal had never done anything like that before (in part because the press doesn't publish male authors). This was an exciting opportunity for the press, and in this case, I knew who Michael Kimmel was and knew he was a bit of a superstar in the world of feminism. Would another press have been interested in this work? Probably not. So it was completely unique and very niche, but oh so right for Seal's list.

The more niche your project, the more likely it is that you're a candidate to publish on a small press. You may have cornered your market. You may be a superstar within your own industry or trade or specialty. Then there are authors who aren't necessarily superstars but have something important to contribute. This could be a historical work or a particular area of study that will contribute to an understanding of something that a select group of people is very interested in reading more about. These authors are also strong candidates for small presses, because small presses often exist to propagate a mission, a deeper understanding of something they value, or good literature.

University presses fit into the small-press profile for this very reason. Many university presses publish trade books and have trade divisions that function almost exactly like small presses. They take on works that have value to them or their lists. They're increasingly publishing more memoir and other mainstream topics, so these are other good avenues to pursue along Publishers Row.

Words of Advice

1. **Consider hiring someone to do the research for you.** There are so many publishers out there that it can become fairly overwhelming to begin digging through them. Unlike agents, most small-press editors don't bother posting their deals on Publishers Marketplace, so that is not a particularly good place to find editors. The best resource I know of is www.lights.ca/publisher, but it's unwieldy, and sorting through it is time-consuming at best, mind-numbing at worst.

2. **Find an editor's name.** Do not submit your work to Acquisitions Editor. It is not difficult to find out whom to submit to at a given press. You can always call the main line and ask who the acquisition editor is. Most often a small press will give you a name, if not an email address and direct line.

3. **Follow submission guidelines.** Make sure you check the guidelines on the publisher's website and do what they ask. Small presses have very clear guidelines, and not following them is good enough reason for an editor not to reply.

Small presses do care about platform, but not nearly as much as big presses do. If you get rejected by agents because of your platform, you need to do some serious thinking about whether you need to take a break and work on your platform, or whether you should pursue a small press instead. Agents understand that they need authors with big platforms, as we discussed in Chapter 4. There will be no big advance on any book that's attached to an author with a minimal platform. Since agents are working on commission, it doesn't make sense for them to pursue a publishing deal for little to no advance. I had an agent who once told me that the project we'd negotiated together was her pro-bono project, because the advance was $5,000, meaning she was getting only $750 up front for all the work she was putting into it. Understandably, agents would prefer to sell books for $50,000 or $100,000 and make a $7,500 or $15,000 commission. And sometimes books with small advances end up earning out their advances, and then there's royalty money to be made. But generally authors publishing on small presses cannot make a living writing full-time.

There are many agents who will drop you if they can't sell your work to a big press. Sometimes this is very matter-of-fact, and it doesn't mean they're a bad agent or that you should hold a grudge against them. It makes sense to me that they sometimes have to cut their losses. But just because you lose your agent doesn't mean your work is done. You just have a different orientation, and you start the process all over again on Publishers Row, hoping to have a meeting of the heart and mind with an editor.

Editors do acquire what they like, what moves them, as long as it fits their list. I had a number of authors over the years approach me in the way that Michael Kimmel and Michael Kaufman did. It didn't often or always work out, but I appreciated authors who felt a burning passion for Seal and who truly believed that their books were a fit for our list. This quickly turned unhappy, however, if they stalked me. It's always okay to pitch. It's never okay to argue with an editor or try to convince them why their rejection of your work was wrongly ascertained. Editors know what they're looking for, and most editors stick to the mantra "I know it when I see it" when it comes to acquiring books. So your primary job is to keep looking for that person who sees *it* in your work.

This is why going to conferences, attending panels, and looking online for editor interviews are all good ways to find out about editors' interests, and to see if you might be able to show them how you can partner with them. At the end of the day, this relationship is always a partnership. An editor should never be doing you a favor by bringing you onboard (and they won't risk their job for that), and you should never assume that your work is bringing something so unique to the press that they cannot move forward without it. You have to showcase how you will work to make taking on your project worth the risk that it inherently is. This is always the mentality an author should have. I'm not suggesting that you have to kiss the feet of your editor and publisher, but if you're an author without much of a platform, or who's bringing a niche project to a small press, you want to enter into this relationship as you would into a business partnership. You don't just dump your project and say good luck or, worse, assume that the publisher is going to get you all kinds of publicity and then feel resentful when they don't. Small presses often don't have the capacity or the relationships to get major media, and so having tempered expectations will ensure that you have a good experience. For most small presses, selling through a print run of five thousand books is considered a success. Many, many books sell through far fewer copies than that.

So with the reality check of small-press publishing firmly in place, let's talk about the pros and the cons of working with one.

Pro #1: Greater likelihood of getting a deal in the first place. Yes, it's easier to get a publishing deal on a small house than on a big house. But you still need to have an amazing book proposal, and you still want to wow the publisher you're trying to work with. Small presses need projects to stay alive in a way that big presses don't because they have their first pick of the lot. I've always espoused that if you stick with it long enough and have enough tenacity, you can get a publishing deal on a small house. But the process can be long and grueling, and it can also require a fair amount of research and figuring out which press is right for your book.

Pro #2: You won't be just another number on a large list. At the big presses, there are generally a select few authors who get all of the resources and attention, meaning that if you're not a lead title (a title that's been determined as worthy of a lot of marketing dollars—usually because of the size of the advance), then it's possible you're not going to get a whole lot of attention from your publicist. At a small press, you can be a big fish in a small pond—and if you fit the profile of a niche author, you can reach your target audience in a way that's satisfying and successful.

Pro #3: More editorial and creative control. Big presses have been known to publish covers without consulting their authors, and sometimes the editorial vision is such that an author wonders what happened to their book. This will never happen at a small press, and you'll weigh in on your title, subtitle, cover design, and interior in a way that a larger house often won't even entertain.

Pro #4: Possibility for a meeting of the heart and mind. In a large house, profits are the bottom line. While one could argue that the death of small presses has to do with the fact that the mission is often the bottom line, the fact that this is true is still a pro, in my opinion. You are very likely to have a relationship with your editor at a small house. The team you'll work with will be tight (and probably very small), and your access to them will usually look much different than it would if you were publishing on a big house.

Pro #5: Realistic expectations. This one is a pro because you want to be working with a team of people who have realistic expectations for what your book can do. If your publisher pays you a $50,000 advance, that means they believe that you'll sell roughly 50,000 copies. This is great if it manifests, but if it doesn't, you can become a pariah. It's highly unlikely that a big publisher will acquire your second book if you don't earn out the advance on your first book. Small presses will consider your book a success if you sell through several thousand copies. Small presses are backlist-driven, meaning that the primary profit they expect to make comes from books that have been around for some time. This is also good news, because a small press is less likely to declare your book out of print than a big press. So your book could be available for years to come on a small press, whereas the same book doing similar sales on a big press could be deemed not valuable enough to keep in print. And now for the cons:

Con #1: Small or no advance and very little marketing budget. Because this is true, you want to be prepared. Set aside some money for marketing and publicity. Many authors who publish on small presses hire their own publicists and create their own marketing opportunities. It's not required, but it's a good idea. Small presses are simply not staffed, nor do they have the budget, to be able to coordinate big marketing campaigns.

Con #2: Less exposure, media, and advertising. This goes hand in hand with small marketing budgets, but it also has to do with the fact that small-press publicists don't have the same media relationships as publicists in big houses. Big houses have relationships that run deep with national media outlets, so when these outlets cover books, they generally consider pitches from the big-house publicists first. That doesn't mean small houses never get national media, but it's rare, and often it's a result of the author's connections, rather than the publicist's.

Con #3: Weaker distribution. It's not unlikely that you won't find your book at the bookstore when you publish on a small press. Many small presses have distribution, but they simply can't get the kinds of buys that big presses can get. Again, this has to do with relationships. Most big presses do their own distribution and have their own sales staff selling the work into the major chains and even to indie bookstores. Most small presses have a third-party distributor, and even when these distributors do a good job of selling a title, the numbers are fractions compared with what big-press sales forces can get.

Con #4: Doing a lot of the work yourself. Because of small presses' limited staff and budget issues, you should be prepared for the journey to begin not when you sell your book, but once your book is published. As I mentioned above, many authors are hiring their own publicists, but even those authors have to work really hard to get themselves in front of audiences. You may be booking your own events, organizing your own tour (local, national, or online), and busting your butt to network and make connections. Some authors love this, but if you're an author who can't even begin to wrap your mind around putting yourself out there in this way, consider yourself forewarned.

Con #5: Realistic expectations. Yes, it's a bit tongue-in-cheek that this is both pro and con #5, but it's for good reason. The downside of realistic expectations is that sometimes small presses don't have the capacity to hold a bigger picture. Occasionally there will be a break-out title on a small press, and sometimes the press itself ends up bungling it because they don't have the staff, expertise, and distribution to see a bestseller through. If your small-press book sees an astronomical rise in sales or gets some sort of major national media attention that launches it into unexpected territory, you'll need to stay on top of your publisher and make sure you're partnering with them, in this case more than ever, as a true business partner would.

Self-Publishing Boulevard: How to Think About Self-Publishing

The biggest thing to know about self-publishing is that there are three primary options: (1) true self-publishing, in which you create a publishing imprint and publish your book under your own imprint name, ISBN, and logo; (2) subsidy publishing (also known as vanity publishing), in which you publish with a third-party entity that publishes and distributes books under their own imprint; and (3) hybrid publishing, which is author-subsidized publishing but generally involves a collaboration with either a traditional press or a self-publishing press that has a particular mission or personal connection to the work you are publishing.

The idea behind "true" self-publishing is that you are the publisher. You function like a small press, whether you publish only your own books or books by other authors. Lightning Source (LSI) is the most known and reliable option when it comes to self-publishing through this model, although LSI allows you to publish only POD (print on demand). If you want to have a short print run, you need to partner with a printer or with a hybrid press that offers that option. When you go the route of true self-publishing, you are independently published and you oversee all aspects of your own book's creation—from editing to proofreading to design, layout, and distribution. Because you also distribute your own book, you have complete control over your product and you don't get a royalty. Instead, you get a net profit on your books, and therefore the more you sell, the more you earn.

True self-publishing is a great option for entrepreneurial authors who intend to publish more than one book, but not the number one choice for authors who have only one book in them, or authors who might need a little more hand-holding. Creating your own imprint means that your books become a business. There are a lot of factors to take into consideration, and a strong comfort level with technology is one of them. LSI is an amazing company, and they're the print-on-demand publisher of choice even for traditional presses, but they're not for everyone. The biggest downside for any newbie author is that they expect you to know what you're doing. They work with traditional publishers and publishers with major lists, and as helpful as their representatives are, they're happy to cut ties if you are an author who needs an education in book publishing basics.

The second option, subsidy publishing, involves working with companies like Author Solutions, as well as the two biggies, CreateSpace (owned by Amazon) and Lulu (founded by Bob Young), that seem to have cornered the market on subsidy publishing (although at the time this book was being written, Kobo had just released its new self-publishing platform, which I'm sure will give CreateSpace and Lulu a run for their money). Subsidy publishers are vendors that make their money by requiring that authors pay for the cost of publication. You own your content, but the company owns the right to distribute your book, and they then pay you a royalty on books sold. There are pros to working with a subsidy publisher, but my general feeling about companies like this is that you're turning over a lot of autonomy. You are publishing under an imprint that's not particularly known for being anything other than a self-publisher. Some of them have good perks. For instance, Lulu's and CreateSpace's direct relationship with Apple and Amazon, respectively, makes it easier for authors to make their works available in the iBookstore and on Amazon generally. Author Solutions offers a lot of author services, including the creation and promotion of authors through websites they build out on behalf of their clients. But it's not particularly specialized. It's templated publishing at its most basic, and once you're published, you keep paying them to continue to get services. There's no particular community of like-minded people whom you're publishing with. You are paying for a service, and the relationship is pretty much that—an exchange of goods for services.

Hybrid publishing offers a solution to this kind of exchange. Hybrid publishers are cropping up all over the place, and included among them are traditional presses that offer hybrid options. There are a number of independent presses who've been hybrid-publishing for years, actually. When I worked at North Atlantic Books, for instance, a number of authors had what was called a "distribution deal," which meant that the entire project was funded by the author but published under North Atlantic's imprint. The royalty, understandably, was weighted heavily in the author's favor, since they were covering the majority of the costs. What North Atlantic has been doing for decades is in fact the model that self-publishers, and especially hybrids, are implementing today.

The idea behind the hybrid is that you subsidize either part or all of your publishing expenses for the privilege (in some cases) or right to publish under a particular imprint. Branding is a big factor in this equation, because the better known the press that's offering these services is, the more gains to the author. The truth is that self-publishing today is no longer stigmatized (in my opinion, at all), but, and this is a big but, it's still very difficult for self-published authors to penetrate a certain level of publicity and media. For many niche authors who don't care about reviews and traditional media, this is a nonissue, but it is an issue for novelists and memoirists and other authors writing on mainstream topics. The media is simply more likely to cover authors who are published on traditional presses. But the hybrid can function as a curtain, giving authors a little more street cred.

So what are these hybrids and how do they work? As I mentioned, some of them are traditional presses. For example, White Cloud Press has been moving to a hybrid self-publishing model and doing it successfully. Others are presses affiliated with traditional presses. Balboa Press, Westbow Press, and Turning Stone Press are examples of these kinds of presses. Balboa and Westbow (though managed by Author Solutions) are directly connected to Hay House and Thomas Nelson, respectively, while Turning Stone Press is an in-house operation that's part of Red Wheel/Weiser. The final category comprises publishing entities like She Writes Press that are not affiliated with a press, per se, but have brand recognition and are connected to a larger community—in this case, a social networking community.

One of the most important things to be said about self-publishing is that you must approach it from a savvy place. Make sure you feel good about your partners. Your own reputation is on the line! Also, hold your head high! As much as the world of publishing has changed in the past five to six years, nowhere has it changed more than in the arena of self-publishing. Self-publishing is a viable and preferred option for many authors. You can get a great return on your investment. If you approach it wisely, you'll probably make more than you would on a traditional house. It's savvy authors who are changing the face of self-publishing. Authors who are taking their work seriously and publishing books that are smart, attractive, and well edited are giving publishers a run for their money. You get to be proud to be a self-published author, and you get to be part of a movement that's changing the rules of publishing.

Words of Advice

1. Do your research! You're going to spend some money to self-publish, so make sure that you really understand what you're getting into. Some self-publishing options are less than transparent, and you want to know why you're paying for the services you're getting. If it's important to you to partner with a press that's affiliated with your values, consider a hybrid press that can offer that. If you care about control above and beyond all else, you should go with LSI. If you have modest expectations and are looking for a self-publisher that will give you a pretty easy and straightforward experience, then a company like CreateSpace or Lulu could be the best option.

2. Know what you're paying for. Some self-publishers offer packages that detail all kinds of services, but if you were to look into it further, you might discover that you could get each of those services à la carte from individual editors, designers, publicists, or web designers cheaper. Self-publishing is not always about getting something for less, of course. As I mentioned, a company's branding or expertise can be quite valuable. But I've also seen self-publishing companies that promote their comprehensive packages in a way that make the packages seem almost irresistible, and yet if you were to drill down you'd discover that a lot of the offerings that are included don't really cost anything to the publisher.

3. Be your own quality control. There should be nothing about your self-published project that indicates to a reader that it's self-published. Some self-publishers are going to make sure you have a beautiful package, and that could be part of your motivation for publishing with them. Others, unfortunately, care less about quality and more about pushing books through their pipeline. The quality of your book matters as much as the quality of your website, or as much as how you present yourself in the world. If you need to hire a consultant to walk you through the various production processes, do. If you don't trust your own design aesthetic, hire someone who can give you some feedback. We've all seen the impact of a poorly designed website. You land and you think, why did you bother? The same is true of a book, and when you're self-publishing, the difference between a mediocre book and a great book is just a matter of going the extra mile and paying a little more money. So it's not a place to skimp.

THE FUTURE OF PUBLISHING

I recently boldly stated that I believe that publishing, within my lifetime, will shift to an exclusively self-published model. I may have been overstating it, since Random House and Simon & Schuster will likely be around forty or fifty years from now (if I'm graced to live that long). But I do believe that the majority of small presses will continue to fold, a trend we've been witnessing since the early 2000s. Small publishing seems to have had its heyday in the 1970s, with the rise of independent publishers and bookstores staking their claims and riding the counterculture wave. Many of them hung on during the '80s and '90s, some of them just barely. Many got acquired by larger presses. Some defied the odds and continue to do their thing. But running a small press, and even a midlevel press, is a tough business.

Author-subsidized publishing looks attractive to publishers who are tired of operating at a loss. I wrote earlier that you as an author are a risk to your prospective publisher. Unless you're truly famous, this is always the case. There is no shoo-in book for the average aspiring writer. Publishers take a gamble when they offer an advance. Even publishers that offer no advance are taking a risk, because publishing a book is expensive. You may be looking at spending somewhere in the realm of $2,500–7,500 to self-publish, but a publisher's numbers don't look that much better. The primary difference is that a publisher takes risks on certain projects knowing it has the power of its moneymaking authors, or its backlist, to keep the press afloat. Big publishers rely on their big-name authors to sell hundreds of thousands of copies to justify their taking risks on lesser-known authors. Small presses rely on the constant, steady payouts from their best backlist sellers to cover the expense inherent in publishing another new list of authors who may or may not earn back in sales what a publisher spends on their book. At both publishers I've worked for, the losses the presses incurred on book after book was a bit sobering.

I believe it is a privilege to be published on a traditional press and a great opportunity to self-publish. And though many people in the publishing world and outside of it mourn what's happening to publishing, I actually see it as a necessary growing pain. There are too many books being published today to sustain the model that publishing of olden days created and to which we still cling. Acquisitions editors are no longer the sole determiners of what will make a successful book. In my opinion, due to the extraordinary emphasis placed on platform, acquisitions editors are actually no longer the deciders of what makes a *good* book. They've instead been trained to assess an author's worth based on how many fans they have, how much publicity they can garner, and what kind of network they're tapped into. On some level, this is fine—these authors can sell books—but we all need to acknowledge and understand that quality gets compromised and there are plenty of self-published books that have more important messages, better writing, and deeper value than the books editors are acquiring on mainstream houses.

There are lots of old-school publishers and editors who think what I'm espousing here is a tragedy. And it is if you've been in the industry forever and you hate the idea of change, or if the notion of the demise of publishing as we know it makes you cringe, or makes you sad. But in my opinion it's not sad, because content is everywhere, and readers are discerning. We will always continue to crave and seek out good content. And publishing houses don't need to be the arbiters of what makes good content. Indeed, I'm arguing now that the majority of them left this discernment at the door in 2000 or earlier.

Our population at large is distributing and consuming content differently than we were one year ago, or even ten years ago. And if we want to be published authors, we need to go with the flow. Your platform matters, but you don't have to be famous. Above and beyond all else, if you have good content that people want, you will find an audience. If you believe you have a message, and if you do the work to find the people who want to hear it, you should publish—no matter what path you choose to pursue. As I write this book, the general state of the publishing industry is quite good. There are still million-dollar deals being signed. There are still auctions and big offers and publishing houses spending thousands of dollars on publicity. There are still surprise runaway-success authors who rise to meteoric heights for reasons that no one can understand. All of these things give the publishing industry a certain aura of mystery and possibility, as I've written about. It's true that you never know, and it's good to have the dream, particularly if it's a motivating dream.

On the flip side, however, there are a slew of books being published every year that are shockingly trite and shallow but tied to huge advances. There is good reason to be discouraged if you're a first-time author shopping for an agent. There are publishers who won't take that risk on you, as much as you work to prove yourself worthy. And plenty of publishing houses are just barely hanging on.

Then there's epublishing, which is big enough to have a chapter of its own. There are agents representing authors who are doing ebook-exclusive deals. There are newbie and well-established authors alike who are taking advantage of the explosion of opportunity in the ebook market. Kindle Singles are, in some cases, selling hundreds of thousands of copies. Since general consumers' capacity for content is notably limited, ebooks offer a way to get your message out in a short format without spending as much money as is required for a print-edition book. On Amazon you don't even need an ISBN or a barcode to get your book up on the site and listed for sale. Talk about low barrier to entry.

The point is that your opportunities are vast, and while the state of traditional book publishing might feel uncertain or unpredictable or on the way down the toilet, the state of publishing at large is healthier and stronger than it's ever been. It's a growth-opportunity industry, much like tech. In fact, publishing has been impacted the way it has been largely because of technology. And so the final takeaway here is that publishing is thriving, and if you haven't already published, it's time to step up and claim your piece of the action. Like publishing in decades past, publishing today is rewarding, exhilarating, and potentially profitable; unlike in decades past, it's now accessible to everyone.

Resources

Publishing Resources

Publishers Marketplace
www.publishersmarketplace.com

This is an industry website, but if you want to find news about agents (who represents whom), publishers (who publishes what), and authors, this is a site you want to at least give a trial run.

Publishers' Catalogues
www.lights.ca/publisher/db/state

A site that allows you to browse publishers by state or city.

Association of Independent Authors
www.independent-authors.org

A resource for self-published authors, including a great database of consultants, editors, and other industry professionals.

Mediabistro
www.mediabistro.com

Sign up for a class, learn exactly what publishers look for in a book proposal, figure out your target readership, and oh so much more. This site has more content than you can ever hope to get through, and it's an amazing resource.

Small Publishers Association of North America (SPAN)
www.spannet.org

I love small publishers, no matter how far I keep moving away from them in my professional life. This site is a helpful resource for marketing your work, complete with lots of industry resources.

The Guide to Literary Agents blog
www.writersdigest.com/editor-blogs/guide-to-literary-agents

1000 Literary Agents
www.1000LiteraryAgents.com

CRWROPPS-B
http://groups.yahoo.com/group/CRWROPPS-B

This is a Yahoo! group open to the public that posts calls for submissions and contest information for writers of poetry, fiction, and creative nonfiction. Just click the JOIN THIS GROUP button and you'll get regular emails announcing all kinds of contests and calls for submissions.

Writing Resources

She Writes
www.shewrites.com

A social networking site for women writers and authors, complete with class offerings and specialized groups dedicated to particular writing and publishing interests.

National Association of Memoir Writers
www.namw.org

An organization that offers teleclasses, telesummits, and tons of professional advice and offerings for memoirists and aspiring memoirists.

NaNoWriMo
www.nanowrimo.org

November is National Novel Writing Month, and this organization will propel you along with your writing—whether you're writing fiction or not.

Bird by Bird: Some Instructions on Writing and Life, by Anne Lamott

An old favorite and highly recommended book about starting small. "Just take it bird by bird."

Self-Editing for Fiction Writers: How to Edit Yourself into Print, by Renni Browne and Dave King

A helpful manual for fiction writers that focuses on writing/editing techniques (the mechanics of dialogue, characterization, point of view, etc.).

Booklife: Strategies and Survival Tips for the 21st-Century Writer, by Jeff VanderMeer

One of the best books I've ever read for writers who are trying to figure out the balance between being a writer and being a self-promoter.

How to Write Attention-Grabbing Query & Cover Letters, by John Wood

A great resource to see what a good query and cover letter should look like.

How to Write a Book Proposal, by Michael Larsen

Written by a well-known Bay Area agent who's got a lot of insider knowledge and tips for doing it right.

The Fast-Track Course on How to Write a Nonfiction Book Proposal, by Stephen Blake Mettee

Written by a small-press publisher who's seen his share of proposals, too.

Architecture of the Novel: A Writer's Handbook, by Jane Vandenburgh

From a Bay Area novelist and memoirist, this book helps writers understand the underlying machinery that propels a plot forward.

Gregory Martin's treadmill journal:
www.unm.edu/~gmartin

Platform Resources

Platform: Get Noticed in a Noisy World, by Michael Hyatt
The best book I've read about platform. Smart, helpful, and thorough!

The Tao of Twitter, by Mark Schaefer
An excellent resource for getting started with Twitter.

Google's Keyword Tool:
adwords.google.com/select/KeywordToolExternal

Twitter: www.twitter.com

Facebook: www.facebook.com

Pinterest: www.pinterest.com

YouTube: www.youtube.com

Google Alerts: www.google.com/alerts

WordPress: www.wordpress.com

GoDaddy: www.godaddy.com

HootSuite: http://hootsuite.com

Seesmic: https://seesmic.com

LinkedIn: www.linkedin.com

Google+: https://plus.google.com

iContact: www.icontact.com

Constant Contact: www.constantcontact.com

MailChimp: http://mailchimp.com

Acknowledgments

First and foremost, thanks to my partner, Krista, who put up with six months' worth of early-morning alarms so I could get the work out. She's been my biggest supporter and a better videographer than either of us could have imagined.

Next, I want to thank all my clients, authors, and readers who supported me along this journey by providing me with accountability. I wouldn't have finished this book in six months if I hadn't stated, out loud and very publicly, that I would and had the championing of so many voices. Thank you so much!

About the Author

© Jen Molander Photography

Brooke Warner is founder of Warner Coaching Inc. and publisher of She Writes Press. Brooke's expertise is in traditional and new publishing, and she is an equal advocate for publishing with a traditional house and self-publishing. *What's Your Book?* is her first book, and she's honored to be publishing on She Writes Press.

Find Brooke online:
www.warnercoaching.com
www.shewritespress.com
www.facebook.com/warnercoaching
twitter.com/brooke_warner
www.pinterest.com/warnercoaching